D1527252

Flight out of Darkness

Military and Athletic Training Tactics to
Strengthen your Spirit and Maintain Peace
on Your Journey

Onnie ReSky

Vitality Tactics L.L.C.
Level One Cross-Check Training

Most Scripture taken from the New King James Version®. Copyright © 1982 by Thomas Nelson, unless otherwise noted, or I forgot to annotate a translation.
Holy Bible, New International Version®, NIV® Copyright ©1973, 1978, 1984, 2011 by Biblica, Inc.®
Amplified Bible. Copyright © 2015 by The Lockman Foundation, La Habra, CA 90631.
The Message. Copyright © 1993, 1994, 1995, 1996, 2000, 2001, 2002 by Eugene H. Peterson

ISBN: 978-1726636681

Dedication

To all those who are still fighting and to remember those that have been lost along the way. No matter where your journey leads you, remember that it matters what you choose to do and be every day.

This book addresses a sensitive subject with a direct approach. It is designed to give techniques and tactics for getting out of darkness when everything else has failed. Sometimes in the midst of chaos and confusion you need things given to you straight, and here it is.

Depression, anxiety, fear...those places of darkness that we can find ourselves in; You need to get out as quickly as possible. Build a plan, get the help you need, whatever it takes. The longer you stay without any forward momentum, the harder it will be to get out. You can become adjusted to the dark and accept less than the abundant life that Christ died to give you.

Keep fighting to get back into the light. It might take several flights to get out and you may have to keep readjusting your plan, but you can do it because of what Christ has already done for you. Get back up.

—Coach Onnie

Contents

Introduction

Sophomore Year, Sijan Hall Cadet dormitory, United States Air Force Academy, 1996: My body hung heavy in the room. My spirit was sinking slowly into a deep, black hole within me. After years of carrying emotional turmoil, the weight of the Academy was causing my fractured insides to crumble. My eyes emptied of hope as my suffocating spirit stared out of the window.

> *"Is any of this really worth the pain you feel right now? How much longer can you continue to hang on like this...Why do this anymore. You can't even feel anything good"*

The mountain view out of my window had lost all beauty and looked more like a prison wall. The dorm room was closing in on me. There were more reasons to quit living, than to keep going. The primary problem was the ongoing chaos within, robbing me of inner peace and self-worth. Nothing had meaning to me, despite having achieved what the world would see as a picture of success. I was attending the United States Air Force Academy; that had to mean I had it all together.

The truth was, I was on the run from a series of abusive situations that spanned several years and had damaged my soul. I had been through physical, emotional and sexual abuse by some of the very people entrusted to care for and mentor me. I smiled and nodded about "my success" in public, but on the inside, I was broken.

God had opened a window of opportunity to escape and it led me to the Academy. I understood enough to know I needed to leave my environment, but I was unequipped to deal with the aftermath of abuse and trauma. I had no knowledge of how to let God heal me. And so, darkness filled the room on my side of the picture frame as the devil saw his opportunity to capitalize on my moment of anguish.

"There is a reason you feel worthless, we both know your truth. There is no way out. Just end it"

At that moment, my mind was flooded with destructive images. Numbness swept through my body and I began to detach from the moment. False promises of freedom from pain and suffering began filling my mind. I couldn't stop seeing the replays of the past as the painful emotions were ripping my spirit apart. My mind was losing the battle as my self-preservation mechanism began to glitch.

About five seconds from failure a song I remembered from Sunday school echoed in my heart: **"Jesus loves me this I know, for the Bible tells me so..."** My mind flashed to a memory of my Grandmother taking me with her to church. The chaos went still as the song trailed off and my spirit took a gasp of air long enough to rise up and snap my mind out of its downward spiral. I stood up, moved on and lived to fly another day.

That was one of my first flights out of darkness that I have a clear memory of. I didn't make it very far away from that dangerous place. But that song playing in my spirit, acted as a rescue mission to pull me back from the edge.

That was not the last time I would be in that nearly defeated state. It seemed like the battles and images were getting more intense and frequent. The enemy was pressing down on me any chance he could get. Any thought I left open in my mind that could be manipulated negatively, he took and tried to use it to destroy me or to create more separation from God.

I often felt confused, distracted and led astray. I couldn't hear God. Despite years of going to church, I did not know Him or His Word very well. In fact, at this time in my life, that Sunday school song was the only thing God could use to reach me. It was He who reached my spirit and pulled me away from the dark thoughts that day. The childhood memory of feeling safe while singing about God's love was still strong enough and still contained enough light, that it could break the negative thought chain.

Time moved on. I graduated from the Academy, then Pilot training, got married, had two children, transitioned from Active Duty to the Reserves, moved to Italy and had a third child. Life in my 20's changed so rapidly I rarely had time for more than a brief thought about where I was in my spiritual life.

In 2005, I found myself living in Italy with three kids under the age of five. Learning how to raise children in a foreign land with no family support was challenging. I was often alone with my children, struggling to make new connections in a foreign environment in my second language.

Again, physical and emotional stress forced me to the edge. Only this time, quitting was not an option. I had built a stronghold in my mind where my parenting responsibilities took away the option to quit. It also sparked motivation to seek peace from my inner turmoil. I was a roller coaster of emotion on the inside, and that made everything more difficult.

I tried really hard to do the right thing every day and be a better parent and person. However, with unresolved conflict and pain inside of me, I couldn't maintain my peace or hold onto joy any longer than a split second. All my efforts fell flat. I accepted and resolved myself to a lowly, but functional existence.

During this time, the devil incessantly attacked my self-worth tempting me into destructive thoughts. Even though I had accepted a spiritually poor existence, he wasn't about to let go of his strategy as long as he could keep making progress on my destruction. In fact, he continued to attack my strength as a parent and almost took me out again in 2013, when he convinced me that even my children would be better off without me.

But for the five years I lived in Italy, my kids still provided enough motivation for me to want to dig deeper into my faith. Although I didn't know Jesus very well, I believed He was my only hope if things were going to get better.

Though I lived in Italy, my spiritual journey had me commuting to Germany for my Air Force Reserve duty. That is where I met an amazing pastor who taught the Word of God in a way I could understand. He was close to my age and American. This made his conceptual references when teaching scripture easier for me to understand. He taught with direct language and straight forward concepts. He also boldly motivated me to do my own reading, memorizing and studying.

He and his wife led regular Bible studies that deepened my knowledge and understanding of Jesus. They were encouraging and provided mentorship in learning how to hear God. They spoke about Jesus like a close, personal friend in their everyday life. They answered any and all questions I had about scripture for years. Their arrival in my life was a blessing and a large reason why I am still "running my race."

My wish is that you live this life to the fullest. The Son of God sacrificed Himself and defeated death so we could have a divine, personal relationship with Him in this life and the next. **"...I have come that they may have life, and that they may have it more abundantly"** (John 10:10). Christ came, lived and died so we could have an abundant life.

My hope is that by sharing my experiences, both difficult and joyous, I can help anyone who is struggling with depression, anxiety, fear or pain in their heart. By studying God's Word, learning to hear His voice, and developing a strategy to strengthen your spirit, I hope you can learn how to have the peace **"which surpasses all understanding"** (Philippians 4:7).

Do not waste the gift of really living by letting your spirit waste away in mere existence. Do not surrender to the enemy. If you are able to read through this book, you still have enough power in you to ignite change. You may not "feel" it, but as an experienced life coach and professional trainer, I guarantee it. You can begin to heal and strengthen your body, mind, spirit, change your course, and make the journey God intended for you.

Let's begin Training

Chapter 1
The Instruction Manual

"Take firm hold of instruction, do not let go; Keep her, for she is your life"
—Proverbs 4:13

Day one of Pilot Training, April 2000—The warm Mississippi air welcomed me to pilot training at Columbus Air Force Base and information overload. An instruction manual for the T-37 aircraft was my first gift. Filled with technical data, systems information and basic operating procedures, it was overwhelming to look at it. The manual was full of monotone writing about basic systems information.

At first glance, I found nothing interesting or inspiring in that book...but I wanted to learn how to fly! I wanted to be a pilot. I had to figure out how to discipline myself to get through all the material and memorize it so they would let me out on the flight line and into an airplane.

As Christians, reading the Bible can be equated to a training requirement. Everyone in the military attends a form of basic training. It is the foundation for being a military member. As Christians, we have a similar form of training available to us in the Bible.

Excitement floods the morning on your first day of pilot training only to be stalled by weeks of academics first. The same beginner's enthusiasm can happen when you initially accept your salvation as a Christian. The instruction and training available on your first and following days is not as well organized for your faith.

We are not always given sound instructional training as we grow. I knew the name of Jesus as a child, but did not understand much about His teachings. I knew that He loved me, but didn't comprehend why or how.

I was almost thirty years old before I understood that my salvation was a gift and I did not have to, nor could I do anything to earn it. How did I attend church off and on all those years and never pick up on that basic piece of information?

Not feeling like a "good enough" Christian held me back from God for many years. It wasn't until I realized that He knew all of me deeply and intimately, still loved me despite that knowledge,

AND He wanted me to have the gift of salvation, that I began to get anywhere. My first thought after that realization was "I just take it? I don't have to keep earning it or be good enough?"

There are a lot of reasons we don't get around to God. Making it a priority in your life to learn His voice, and develop a cross-check of including Him in everything is <u>the one thing</u> that will help you in all areas of life.

To begin your journey or learn how to sharpen your existing skills, you must make the Bible a regular study. It is a living book and its contents provide an abundance of information for life skills and guidance that are critical to mature as a Christian.

As with any ability, there are different levels of mastery. As a pilot, the more you know and comprehend about your aircraft, the better equipped you are to handle it and any problems that occur. The exact same thing is true as a Christian; the more time and effort you put into studying, the better you will get at extracting wisdom and applying scriptural knowledge for the problems you might encounter.

Required Reading

"But He answered and said, 'It is written, Man shall not live by bread alone, but by every word that proceeds from the mouth of God'"
—Matthew 4:4

Reading God's Word is an essential procedure to maintaining a growing and maturing relationship with Christ. It is a foundational document for being able to hear His voice and recognize when He is talking to you. By knowing what He has already said in His Word, you can begin to decipher what He sounds like in your life.

Have you ever heard someone tell you that your best friend said something, but you didn't believe them because it didn't sound like something your best friend would say? Normally you at least ask your best friend about it before you make any judgements about what they supposedly said. Based on their history and your relationship with them, you are familiar with "how they sound" and what you know them to think and say.

The same is true with God. Once you are familiar with His Word, you are more easily able to identify his voice and recognize His spirt. You are able to recognize when scripture has been taken out of context and misapplied to a situation. Just as your friend may have been taken out of context or information was missing, the same can happen with God's Word. This further highlights the importance of having your own regular study of the Bible and growing relationship with God.

Go All In

"For everything that was written in the past was written to teach us, so that through the endurance taught in the Scriptures and the encouragement they provide we might have hope"
—Romans 15:4 (NIV)

The Bible is a historical document, and a Christian life instruction manual written by the one who created us so that we have what we need to make it through this life with hope and encouragement. It can seem overwhelming to read at first. However, God did not give us something we are not capable of understanding or comprehending. He is an excellent teacher to any willing student.

Being mentally present, engaged in learning and open to hearing His instruction quicken the learning. There may be parts of the Bible you do not find interesting. However, I recommend you read through them at least once. This will help you construct a stronger foundation of understanding.

I understand not being enthusiastic about adding the discipline of scripture study into your life. I often did not feel like memorizing material for flying. I needed a different perspective on studying to keep me motivated. For pilot training, I wanted to graduate! The fear of failure moved me to find the time I needed to be successful.

No matter what phase of life you are in, scripture study will help you be more successful. When you give time to God, you receive more back in terms of wisdom and understanding. You will have more peace and make better decisions in life. The relationship growth and increasing efficiency makes the time invested well worth it.

Building a strong, well-developed faith takes time. However, by adding even one or two of the right scriptures at the right moment, to stand on in your faith, will be very powerful. **"the word of God is quick, and powerful, and sharper than any two-edged sword"** (Hebrews 4:12). I recommend adding daily study as soon as possible. Even five minutes a day will be worth your effort.

Note: Before beginning to study, firmly decide whether you accept the Bible as a divinely written document. If you are prone to doubt its authenticity, go and find the proof you need to make an informed decision. Check out how the document's integrity has stood the test of time against other ancient works. The first book I recommend is "The Case for Christ," by Lee Strobel. Now a movie, but of course the book is more comprehensive. I also went through "How We Got The Bible" by Neil Lightfoot. Believing that what you read is truth is critical for building a strong foundation in your faith.

Notes, Cautions, and Warnings

An aircraft manual has notes, cautions and warnings added throughout the text to highlight important supplemental information. In this book *Notes* will highlight or expand on information already given, or they will offer tips on easier operation and further understanding.

For example, the book of proverbs has many insightful notes for life. One of my favorite proverbs: **"Never correct conceited people; they will hate you for it. But if you correct the wise, they will respect you."** (Proverbs 9:8 GNT). Have you ever corrected someone who seems to know everything and seen the way they react? The information is rarely received, and usually causes dissention between you and them. Meanwhile, a wise person corrected in a humble manner will respect you for the insight you provide them.

Cautions highlight an operating procedure or practice, which if not strictly observed, could result in damage to or destruction of equipment or loss of mission effectiveness. Cautions in this book refer to things that are important to emphasize for health or safety.

*Warnings** highlight an operating procedure or practice which, if not correctly followed, could result in personal injury or loss of life. They emphasize information of immediate flight safety importance. In the flying world we are told that warnings are written in blood. Someone probably lost their life for the information to have made warning status. In this book, warnings carry the same importance.

Procedure versus Technique

As an Air Force pilot, I was taught how to fly by the best. By studying procedures and learning techniques from other experienced pilots I went from zero flying knowledge to trained pilot. Many of these same training concepts of using procedures and techniques can be applied when learning how to use scripture to fly in life.

A procedure is something in the flying world that is non-negotiable. It must be done precisely. For example, an aircraft has a starting sequence. It must be started in the same order each time.

Techniques are negotiable, they work for some pilots but not others. Sometimes they can help you remember procedures. In general, they can help, but never hurt to try.

In this book I will give you procedures to follow that are based on scripture. Then I will list out some techniques that have worked for me and might for work you. The procedure is scripture based and will not change, the Word of God is non-negotiable. The technique is a starting point for you to try if you need direction implementing the procedure. Sometimes, I will provide a personal demonstration to illustrate the technique further. I will also include notes, warnings and cautions about concepts along the way.

"My people are destroyed for lack of knowledge"
—Hosea 4:6

This scripture fascinates me. This is God speaking about His own people. He is saying that Christians can be destroyed by their lack of knowledge. Woah! Stop and think about that for a moment. This should not be since God will give wisdom freely to all those who ask:

"If any of you lacks wisdom, let him ask of God, who gives to all liberally and without reproach, and it will be given to him."
—James 1:5

Flying is awesome, but without the right knowledge you can get yourself and/or others into a life-altering or ending situation. Our Christian lives have a similar parallel. Without dedicated study and practice applying the Word of God, we are not going to experience the life He designed for us.

The consequences of that range from a dull ache longing for something you can't understand, or a life full of emptiness, and all the way to the tragic: A life wasted or a soul lost to an eternity of separation from God. Without the developed ability to hear and listen for God, we can end up in the wrong places at the wrong time.

The Word of God vs. Your Feelings

"Jesus loves me this I know, for the Bible tells me so..." It's interesting to look at the first line of this Sunday school song and break it down. First, it factually states that Jesus loves you. Then, it bases that knowing on divinely written truth. It never mentions anything about your feelings.

As you read the Word of God there are going to be times when His Word disagrees with how you feel. For example, you might feel like you are alone and God is not with you. However, this scripture would contradict that feeling:

> **"...For He Himself has said, 'I will never leave you nor forsake you.'"**
> —Hebrews 13:5

Technique: Toss all negative emotions or thoughts that are contrary to God's Word. You are loved, forgiven, accepted, and always wanted. Our feelings fluctuate, God does not.

You are Designed to Hear

Did you know that we are designed with the ability to hear God's voice? I remember my first run-in with the statement, "We can all hear God's voice." My initial response was, "but God doesn't talk to me." Then, after listening to various sermons by Pastor Keith Moore, I learned that there are pre-requisites.

The first pre-requisite is a ready and willing heart to do what He says. So, I asked myself if I had a willing heart to follow His guidance. The truth was, I was scared of what He might ask me to do. I needed more trust in the relationship before I would be ready to open up.

Know the condition of your heart. Are you willing and ready to accept instruction from God? If your heart is not open, you will have difficulty hearing God and it will be even harder to do what he says.

*Warning: When you begin to recognize that you are hearing God, but opt not to do something He tells you to, this is also called rebellion...which can lead to getting ourselves lost or being in harm's way.

Moore also advises that you stop saying that God doesn't speak to you. You could be interrupting the Holy Spirit while He's trying to talk to you! With an open mind and a ready ear, you are now prepared to start studying the Word of God.

Procedure: Listen for Gods voice to guide your life decisions

"My sheep hear my voice, and I know them, and they follow me."

—John 10:27-28

"Hearing God" does not always mean an audible sound in your ears. It can, but that is not usually the case. This term is used to include the many ways God will communicate with us. It is a descriptive phrase for how God reaches us in our hearts. There are times He will use another person to deliver a message, a circumstance of opportunity, a coincidence of choice. The methods of delivery and communication are as creative as He is.

What makes these moments similar is how it rings through your spirit when you KNOW what happened was for you. Those experiences have the ability to freeze time and leave your heart standing still. The air clears as God's truth, direction, or answers you seek, transmit straight through your heart.

God also speaks to us and guides us through incredible timing and favorable situations. But not always! This is why it is important to learn to decipher His voice. Have you ever had a person call you that you know, but it takes a moment to recognize their voice on the phone? Sometimes it takes a couple of sentences for you to confirm their identity. Be vigilant and clear minded when listening, the devil also uses people and circumstances.

Technique: Regularly study God's Word to train your ear to hear His voice. When I set my mind on hearing God, I would remember John 10:27-28, and repeatedly say "I hear the voice of the shepherd" Saying scripture out loud plants it in your heart. I would repeat this multiple times to develop the confidence that I could hear God speak to me. I stopped saying "I can't hear God" and "He doesn't speak to me." He said I could hear Him and I stopped disagreeing with Him.

Still not convinced He speaks to us or you can hear Him? I would like to gently present this scripture:

"He who is of God hears God's words; therefore you do not hear, because you are not of God."
—John 8:47

Ouch. Now, I am not saying you are not of God. I am presenting this scripture in support of the fact that as a child of God, you are designed to hear from God and that He does speak to us. Based on scripture, the only people who do not hear God, are those who are not His.

Therefore, if you are of God and have not experienced hearing from Him, consider opening your mind to the idea that you simply have not trained your ear. Try thinking of this as an area of your spiritual life that you have yet to develop. The important thing to know is that you can hear God because you are designed to. Changing your approach and training can open your mind and enable your ears.

"He who has ears, let him hear" repeated in Matthew 11:16, Matthew 13:9, Mathew 13:43, Mark

4:9, Mark 4:23, Luke 8:8, Luke 14:35, Revelation 2:7, Revelation 2:11, Revelation 3:6, Revelation 3:13, Revelation 13:9

I encourage you to **"Study to shew thyself approved unto God, a workman that needeth not to be ashamed, rightly dividing the word of truth."**
—2 Timothy 2:15

Reading scripture is equivalent to listening to a conversation that God has recorded for our use. You begin to learn his nature. For example, in Hebrews 11:6 you *hear:*

"But without faith it is impossible to please Him, for he who comes to God must believe that He is, and that He is a rewarder of those who diligently seek Him."

The first time I read Hebrews 11:6, I wondered what He meant when He wrote it. Isn't it "bad" to do something seeking a reward? Shouldn't I just seek God because I'm supposed to, because he told me to, because it's the "right" thing to do?. . . It felt wrong to do something expecting a reward.

However, this is what God wanted me to know about His nature. He is a rewarder. Why am I arguing with what He wanted me to know about Him? So, when the road gets rough seeking God, I remember that

He is a rewarder to those who diligently seek Him, and it gets a little easier. This is not all for nothing.

Note: This is only one example of why we seek God. You will find many others as you learn about Him.

At the beginning, my trust and faith to be able to hear God was small due to lack of experience. Solution: I prayed for more faith and for God to show me how to develop my trust in Him. Here are some techniques that I used to begin scripture training:

Technique #1: Break up reading the Bible into smaller readings everyday till you make it through in its entirety. I recommend reading the Bible through front to back at least one time in your life. Hey, it's a very long-running, international best-seller, you should check it out!

I prefer a Bible where the old testament has been put in chronological order. This made it easier for me to follow. I recommend the King James version as the best translation there is. However, the New King James version reads friendlier.

Use online resources such as biblegateway.com to change the translation version of the same scripture to help you when the meaning is not clear to you. Change the version three or four times until you can grasp the full meaning. For example, the Amplified Bible is an excellent resource for expanding on additional equivalent meanings of key words from the original Hebrew and Greek texts. I used "The Message" translation frequently in the beginning of my studies. I could almost always understand a complex scripture illustrated by this version that uses a very simple conversational tone.

Demo: Here is an example of the same scripture changed into four different translations. Notice how they say the same thing, but in a different way.

King James: **"For God so loved the world, that he gave his only begotten Son, that whosoever believeth in him should not perish, but have everlasting life."**

New King James: **"For God so loved the world that He gave His only begotten Son, that whoever believes in Him should not perish but have everlasting life."**

The Amplified Bible: **"For God so [greatly] loved and dearly prized the world, that He [even] gave His [One and] [a]only begotten Son, so that whoever believes and trusts in Him [as Savior] shall not perish, but have eternal life."**

The Message: **"This is how much God loved the world: He gave his Son, his one and only Son. And this is why: so that no one need be destroyed; by believing in him, anyone can have a whole and lasting life. God didn't go to all the trouble of sending his Son merely to point an accusing finger, telling the world how bad it was. He came to help, to put the world right again. Anyone who trusts in him is acquitted; anyone who refuses to trust him has long since been under the death sentence without knowing it."**

—John 3:16

Technique #2: Commit to knowing key scriptures for spiritual development. Memorizing scripture will plant it in your heart and you will begin to know the voice of God. It is similar to hearing or knowing things your best friend would say or do in a situation, or how you can sometimes hear your parents in your thoughts.

Demo: A pastor once challenged me to say the Pauline prayers (Ephesians 1:16-23, Ephesians 3:14-21, Philippians 1:9-11, and Colossians 1:9-14) out loud every day for 30 days to see what would happen. I accepted and completed the challenge. Shortly after completing the experiment I had the first sign of its effects.

I was checking out at the grocery store and the person bagging my groceries began to make comments that made me uncomfortable. I wanted to get out of there as fast as I could. As soon as I paid, I walked quickly ahead of her to avoid a conversation. On the way to my car, the words "rooted and grounded in love" rang through my spirit. By the time we reached my car, I was able to turn around and be pleasant to the woman who had made me so uncomfortable.

By spending time speaking the scriptures out loud, they had become planted in my heart. The Lord was then able to use them at the appropriate time to course correct me. What I found is the scriptures began to echo in my spirit. The Holy Spirit was able to use them to correct or encourage me when I needed it. You can download a copy of the Pauline Prayers for your training at: vitalitytactics.com

Technique #3: Find experienced mentors and/or teachers to help you begin and continue your studies. In the military we have experienced instructors to train students on the same path they have taken. Beyond reading the entire manuscript, seek out knowledgeable teachers of the Word. Listen to sermons online, find a good local preacher, or have some type of guided daily devotional practice. There are several different preachers or organizations that will send daily devotionals to your email.

My favorite Bible teachers for sermons include:

Keith Moore – He has a life-giving sermon series on how to hear Jesus. Go to his website: moorelife.com and download the series "Seeing Jesus"

Jesse Duplantis – This guy is hysterical. He comes from a relatable rebellious past, had a temper to overcome and is a great story teller. Check out his video series "A Merry Heart Doeth Good like A Medicine"

Andrew Wommack – A great Bible teacher that is good at putting things in direct and simple to understand ways.

Joyce Meyers – She was instrumental in explaining to me how to live everyday life with scripture as a foundation for guidance.

Joseph Prince – This man is a scripture genius. He expertly weaves scripture from old and new testament together to give you an in-depth and solid foundation on topics. This is also who I receive my daily email devotionals from.

Technique #4: Practice using scripture in challenging situations before they occur. In pilot training we practice our missions beforehand by chair flying. We sit in a chair, normally in front of a cockpit mockup, and practice going through the entire mission. From start-up, taxi, take-off, the entire flight lesson expected, through engine shut down, all in our minds. We think through and imagine running checklists, visually locating where the switches are, and things we anticipate we will say on the radio.

If you have a tough day coming up, practice it in your mind. Consider when you might be in a difficult moment and ask God for help with it. See yourself maintaining balance and your power throughout normally difficult or task saturated moments. Find scriptures that might directly apply to what you anticipate your needs will be. An internet topic search on scriptures on peace, wisdom, or courage will quickly yield suggestions that can help.

Technique #5: During pilot training we also have group study sessions. As students we gather to learn from each other, encourage one another, and struggle together. Small groups in your Christian life can be essential to keeping yourself mentally and physically strong.

You will also develop a community of support for when life becomes challenging. Many of your local churches will have small groups available to join.

They can be organized by marital status, age, or with certain goals. Pick one with a topic that resonates with your heart or that you find interesting.

Technique #6: Reread known scriptures with an open mind for additional or new insights. The Bible is a living book. Depending on what phase of life or mindset you are in, you will get different things out of the same story.

For example, the parable of the prodigal son, Luke 15:11-32. For years I heard this story as focused on the prodigal son. He returns home after he decides to take his inheritance early and leave the family for riotous living. The other son stays and works hard for his father. After some time passes the prodigal son returns and the father receives him with open arms and a welcome-back party.

Traditionally this story is told as one to illustrate God's forgiveness when receiving us back after we have lived rebelliously. However, another lesson can be found. The story of the faithful son. He was jealous that the father rejoiced and celebrated the return of the prodigal son.

The faithful son was resentful that the father was giving to the other child because he had worked so hard all this time. The father's answer was **"...Son, you are always with me, and all that I have is**

yours" (Luke 15: 31). The lesson? The faithful son was trying to earn favor from his father by his works, not realizing he was with him daily and already had access to everything that belonged to his father.

How often do we find ourselves trying to work hard for God's blessings when we already have them through Christ's sacrifice on the cross? We do not have the ability to earn them, they are given to us.

I urge you to begin studying as soon as possible. Even if you only have two minutes that you can dedicate to reading a devotional that is sent to your email daily. Start there and build. Pick two of the techniques above to start using today. List the ones you've chosen here, or print the worksheet "Level-one Cross-Check training" at vitalitytactics.com. Fill it out and keep it in plain view in your office or home:

1.

2.

Chapter 2
Know your Jet

The U.S. Air Force arguably has the best system in the world for making pilots. As a student pilot, you spend weeks in a classroom studying aircraft systems, flight regulations, instrument flying, aerospace physiology, navigation, flight planning and aviation weather...all without getting to touch the aircraft. We weren't allowed in the jet until we had a basic knowledge of how it and the operational environment we would fly in worked.

We learned it is important to be able to understand what your aircraft instruments can tell you about your flight situation by looking at them. In a cockpit, you see multiple readouts on engine RPM, airspeed, heading, altitude, etc. You must be able to interpret the data at a glance and make decisions.

In pilot training, the first thing you learn is what the instruments are SUPPOSED to say. What are the normal operating limits? Next, you learn what it means if they are above or below those limits and the procedures for correcting the condition. Our body, mind and spirit also have indicators that we can learn to interpret to understand our current situation and identify potential problems before they become emergencies.

Many of the same principles used in the flying world also work for maintaining flight in your personal life. As a pilot, you trust the engine instruments to give your current status so you can make decisions for the next phase of flight. As a human, when you know the current condition of your spiritual state, your mental health and your physical condition, you can make better decisions about your day and long-term goals.

Then, if you identify a readout that is not within limits you can begin trouble shooting the problem. For example, if your spirit is low, you can learn techniques to bring it back to a state of peace. But until you learn your normal operating limits and regular maintenance needs, you will struggle to maintain balance and make noticeable progress in any one direction.

Note: The body, mind and spirit all have a directing force in your life. However, the body and mind should be in service to our Spirit that is God led.

Every day you wake up and take flight. Who or what is guiding you on your journey? Is it your own desires? That does not have to be all bad if those decisions were the ones formed in you by God: **"Delight yourself in the Lord, and He will give you the desires of your heart"** (Psalm 37:4). When we enjoy our relationship with God and regularly spend time with Him, our desires become shaped by Him.

You are influenced by who you hang out with. You will begin to absorb their thoughts and beliefs as your own, or strengthen what you already know. Choose wisely.

Who is flying your jet?

We have free will and can let anyone, anything or set of beliefs take the controls. What voice and set of beliefs guides you every day? Your daily practices reflect who you lean on for guidance. For example, if your career ambitions are dictating your life choices, it could be a sign of the ego driving. Continuing that path reinforces those values and you become the expert at that way of life.

Perhaps family or spouse considerations are the predominant force. Although this sounds better than your ego, it also is not the best solution. Keeping

God in charge of your plan will allow everything to fall into place. He knows you have a career and a family to consider. Trust Him to line up the day's priorities for you. Develop a daily routine of checking in with God about what He has planned for you.

Technique: Find a space that is quiet and allows you to be still for a moment. In prayer, ask God how He would divide your time during the day. Ask Him to prioritize your daily task list for you. What do you feel Him telling you to do first?

Learn Your Instrument Panel and How you are Wired

All humans have similar basic needs; food, water and shelter, but we are also uniquely designed. Through trial and error we learn about our individual likes, dislikes, allergies, sleep patterns, spiritual needs, etc. Pay attention to your body, and the thoughts and emotions that run through you every day. Then you can begin to correlate results to the actions you are choosing.

The body, mind, and spirit all live together, occupying the same spaces. One will affect the other. For example, a person who is sad might make mentally different choices than they would have if they had been in a happier mood. When you become hungry, you might have a shorter temper. When you are stressed, you might eat more while someone else loses their appetite.

The Body

Procedure: **"I discipline my body like an athlete, training it to do what it should. Otherwise, I fear that after preaching to others I myself might be disqualified."**

—1 Cor 9:27 (NLT)

When left unchecked without healthy boundaries and regular discipline, I equate the body to an undisciplined toddler. It can become unruly, demanding and begin to dictate your life. Give into any of it's whims without boundaries for long enough, and you can soon become a slave to its demands to stay comfortable. From physical cravings to never feeling like doing anything but sitting on the couch, you must discipline your flesh so it does not have more of a say than it needs to in your decision making.

Get to know your body. People assume that since I exercise regularly that my body does not resist me. That is not true. Most of the time my body votes no to exercise. It has no interest! However, mentally and spiritually I feel renewed and happier after I have finished exercising. And even though it hates to admit it, my body also feels better after it is done. Yet, it will still have no interest once it is time to exercise again. I have had to develop a mental strength of focusing on the after feeling to get my body to the gym. Half the battle is showing up.

Maintain a solid exercise, nutrition and sleep schedule for two weeks. Then, begin altering things one a time to see what works best for you. Increase your exercise to a minimum of 30 minutes every day and see how that effects your sleep and mood. Avoid excess sugar. Maybe eliminate dairy for one week to see if it affects you in any way. After maintaining a solid routine for two weeks, pick three things to either stop doing or start doing for your body and document the effects here or on your Cross-Check panel:

1.

2.

3.

The Mind

Procedure: "...whatever is true, whatever is noble, whatever is right, whatever is pure, whatever is lovely, whatever is admirable—if anything is excellent or praiseworthy—think about such things... and the God of peace will be with you"

—Philippians 4:8

Get to know your mind. What belief or thought will be stronger in your mind 10 years from now because you think about it every day? Write down the 3 thoughts that repeat most often in your mind and evaluate their effectiveness. How you can improve them to better serve your purpose?

1.

2.

3.

What happens when the thoughts are incessantly negative? It can physically harm you. For example, negative thoughts and emotions can trigger a cortisol release in the body. The problems associated with elevated levels of cortisol for long periods of time include: anxiety, depression, digestive problems, headaches, heart disease, sleep problems, weight gain and memory/concentration impairment. This is an example of the mind affecting the body.

The Spirit

Procedure: To know the condition of your heart, monitor the words that come out of your mouth. "... **For out of the abundance of the heart his mouth speaks**"

—(Luke 6:45).

Get to know your spirit. Pay attention to how often your words are positive or negative. Do you build people up or tear them down? Are you kind, forgiving and respectful with your speech? Do you feel peaceful most of the time? Are you able to recover from adverse stimuli in a reasonable amount of time? Is it comfortable and easy for you to enjoy life and be happy for others when they have success?

Evaluate yourself for the presence of the fruits of the spirit:

"...love, joy, peace, longsuffering, kindness, goodness, faithfulness, gentleness, self-control..."
—Galatians 5:22-23

Which ones are missing or do you want more present in your life?

Clarify it here:

1.

2.

3.

Train Hard, Train Smart, No Matter Where You Begin From

No matter where you find yourself you can always get closer to God and know Him more. It will only benefit you to let Him into your life more and more. How do we manage studying the Word of God, learning about ourselves and growing closer to God along the way? You start from wherever you are and train yourself to the next level.

One of my initial flights of trust with God, occurred while I was living in suburban Italy. In 2005, I found myself a stranger in a strange land with a small family. Life as an expatriate can deliver some hard transitions that you never expected. Everything I knew had been yanked out from under me.

Planning what to eat for dinner, finding the ingredients, reading and communicating in Italian, and getting it all ready with three little ones running around was overwhelming. It was driving the homesickness deep into my heart. Night after night, deciding on dinner became more difficult as the continued stress of the situation was depleting me.

Procedure: **"If any of you lacks wisdom, let him ask of God, who gives to all liberally and without reproach, and it will be given to him. But let him ask in faith, with no doubting, for he who doubts is like a wave of the sea driven and tossed by the wind"**

—James 1:5-6

I began to pray. I asked God what I should make for dinner. Then I would listen to my heart. I would do my best to be absolutely silent for a moment and try to hear something in my spirit. The first thing I heard, I would go with it. It worked well for the first couple of nights. Then, I began to doubt myself. Was I really hearing God? What if that was my subconscious just throwing things out there? Did the

God of the entire universe really care about my dinner dilemma?

Procedure: **"Casting all your care upon Him, for He cares for you"**

—1 Peter 5:7

Then, I started to judge myself about what was worrying me. First world whining? Why am I wasting God's time? But for whatever reason, that is where I found myself in life. Trying to organize what was for dinner every night was one of the things keeping me bogged down in my spirit and causing frustration. I also identified this as an area where I was able to begin to exercise my faith more.

Faith requires action on things unseen. Praying about dinner seemed like the first flight of trust, faith, and listening that I was capable of making at that time in my life. Although not very far or high, it was my first intentional flight of faith with God.

"But the very hairs of your head are all numbered…"
—Luke 12:7

I decided that if He's numbering the hairs on my head, then he cares about me and what I am struggling with, no matter how small. I understood that building a relationship with God required talking to Him about everything that was bothering me. If something upset me, no matter how small, I began praying about it.

So, I humbled myself and went with it. I asked God daily for help in deciding what to make for dinner. Sometimes I would even do contrary to what I heard just to see what happened. Often nothing important would happen, but usually I could see how what I had heard would have gone better. I used the recurring dinner decision conversation to sharpen my ear to distinguish between a suggestion from my own thoughts and God's direction.

Dinner planning began to flow more smoothly as the months passed. I learned to differentiate between my own thinking and promptings from the Holy Spirit. I grew in the comfort that God was there to help me. My tiny problem did matter to Him. It was a comforting flow as I experienced a small revelation of scripture in my life.

Technique: Learn to trust God when he speaks to your heart. Build the relationship by starting with situations you need help with and are able to let go of the outcome. Find the area in your life that you can relinquish control of and trust Him with. Pray, and then be ready to hear. I urge you to begin practicing this regularly as soon as possible. Like any new skill, it will not be perfect in the beginning. Do not worry about messing it up. Just keep going! You are not going to get better until you are consistent in your efforts.

Note: One of the biggest distractors to hearing God is your own flesh. You must learn to create peace within yourself. Sometimes at a moment's notice and in the midst of chaos. Learning to zone in on the spirit when there is chaos around you takes practice!

*Warning: You need to be able to hear God in Emergency situations, it could be the difference between life and death for you or someone else one day. The key take away from this, is you want and need this skill when life gets hard. You do not want to be in an intense situation that requires critical, possible life altering or ending decisions, and not be able to hear God because you can't focus. The only way I could develop the ability to hear in a tense situation was to practice building trust with God under less stressful conditions. It's the difference between receiving guidance while flying straight and level in calm weather, and maintaining straight and level in turbulence with unexpected thunderstorms. Learn how to do it in the calm before you need it during a storm.

Starting with small, simple questions or needs that have little consequence in case you misinterpret what you hear will create a calmer training environment to learn in. Trust takes time to build in a relationship. Try things you are comfortable trusting to a stranger.

For example, when you first arrive in a new city you would ask anyone on the street that you feel comfortable speaking to, for a local restaurant recommendation. Even though you don't know them, you will take their word for it.

The worst thing that can happen is you get a bad meal. However, a recommendation improves the odds that you will have a great meal. There is no real loss if what you hear is not accurate or true.

Conversely, you would not ask this person how to invest your life savings. Without knowing their credentials or financial background, you would not hand over that decision to an unqualified stranger. Until you know God more deeply and are able to trust Him on a regular basis with your life decisions, you're unlikely to take bigger risks with Him in charge.

Logically, we know that trusting God with everything is a wise decision. He is all knowing and loves us more than we can comprehend. The actual doing of that takes growing in our spirit and disciplining our flesh.

Note: God always gives us more than we ask for

My dinner planning experience led me to open my heart more and stand on different scriptures in the expectation that God does what He says He will. Unexpectedly, a few months later, a colleague walked into the office one day with books to give away. She was moving and getting rid of things. She asked me if I wanted any of the books she brought in. Amongst the pile the book titled "Saving Dinner" caught my eye. I knew I was supposed to take it.

It was a book full of basic recipes. The difference between this cook book and others is that it organized an entire week of evening meals for you by providing the shopping list, then the recipes that corresponded to the lists. It made my life so much better to learn this skill. I didn't even know a resource like this existed.

I had asked for help with deciding what was for dinner each night. God answered that prayer, then sent the information on how to organize my week. The recipes in that book were not complicated and easy for me to use. I spent the next year learning how to cook out of that book.

After a year, my cooking skills grew tremendously. I went from being stressed, not knowing how to organize and feed a family, to a prepared and educated cook able to have dinner on the table each night. God had more than answered my daily prayer. That experience was my first intentional attempt to strengthen my ability to hear God and it also strengthened my faith.

Fly Higher

After spending time studying God's Word and planting it in my heart, I became more adept at listening and doing. As a result, I wanted to experience more of God. I still felt a distance. I was only involving Him in the smaller parts of my life and not utilizing faith for much more than relieving low level stress and worry.

I then heard a sermon by Joyce Meyers where she said, "God will get as close to you as you want, it's not Him that is holding the relationship back." That thought rang through my soul. I became really curious what that would mean for my life. Why wouldn't I want to be as close to God as possible? He is Love and all things amazing.

A clear prayer erupted from my heart "Lord, help me learn how to be closer to you. Show me how to get rid of whatever is blocking me from becoming closer to You"

I said that prayer at the end of 2013. Although I considered myself actively engaged in God's Word, the sadness in me at that point of my life was almost unbearable. I was living in Germany, had an amazing job, healthy children, was financially secure, and I felt awful that I couldn't just be happy. I was so blessed!

There was a problem somewhere in my life causing me pain. I cried out to God for help and I didn't even know what for, but I knew He did. The answer I received back was "Go teach exercise classes." I had no idea what that meant. I was sad, and He wanted me to teach exercise classes?... that made no sense.

Note: You will not always immediately get the answers to the questions you ask God. However, I can guarantee that He will never give you the information late. You might miss it if you aren't listening, but the answers come before you need them. Never have I had God tell me, *Oh yeah, I forgot to tell you something last week. It totally slipped my mind.*

Procedure: **"His mother said to the servants, Whatever He says, do it"**

—John 2:5

That is one of the best pieces of advice I can pass along. Spoken by Mary, the mother of Jesus, at a wedding. The after party had run out of wine and the disciples were asking Jesus what to do about it. He told them to go fill up the water pots with water.

Logically, that made no sense. They were out of wine, not water. Why the heck would they go do that? Instead of asking Him questions or complaining, they just did what He said. Unbeknownst to them, they were about to become part of the first recorded miracle Jesus performed in the New Testament...the turning of water into wine.

Note: I would like to point out this was not healing the sick or helping the poor. The first recorded miracle was at a party...they asked for party supplies. He responded by delivering the best wine. This speaks to God's interest in caring for all our needs. He is a loving God and has no problem with us celebrating and having fun. Some of my greatest adventures with God were also a lot of fun.

So, I took Mary's advice. I had no idea why I needed to teach exercises classes, but I knew it was clearly what God had told me to do. I had to overcome my flesh though. It was full of self-doubt, fear, and laziness. It in no way, wanted anything to do with what God had asked.

Being led by my spirit, I walked into my local gym and volunteered to teach group exercise classes. Somehow that turned into teaching twice a day 4-5 times a week for 6 weeks. This happened to coincide with my involvement in a military exercise that required long days and lots of new learning.

My brain was shocked right out of the destructive thought patterns I didn't even realize it was in. The intense uptake in physical exercise and constant influx of new information at work put my depressed brain on a different wave length, changed my body chemistry, strengthened my body and set me up for the next step in my healing...signing up for Ironman Austria in 2014.

For those unfamiliar with the Ironman race: This is a 140.6 mile course. In one day you must swim 2.4 miles, bike 112 miles, and run 26.2 miles. There is an overall time limit of 17 hours to complete. Each phase also has cutoff times you must meet or you are not allowed to continue and be an official Ironman finisher.

The idea sounded completely crazy to me, but my spirit couldn't let it go. I received a charity invitation to race in Ironman Austria which was coincidentally only one week after I was due to race in my first Half Ironman in Aarhus, Denmark. My flesh was adamant, there is no way you are supposed to race your first full Ironman one week after a 70.3 Ironman.

I waffled back and forth on the idea for days. Finally, I felt I heard clearly that it was God telling me to do it. Six weeks before the race was to start, I paid the entry fee and signed up for Ironman Austria. My first attempt at completing 140.6 miles of swimming, biking and running.

Once I completed the signup, I had complete peace in my spirit. For me, peace in my spirit is a confirmation that the message was from God. However, my flesh began to freak out.

But there were confirmations along the way that helped me grow emotionally stronger as the race approached. In my heart, God gave me the idea to dedicate my first Ironman race to my step-mother. I wanted to give her the finishers medal.

Her medical issues at the time did not allow her to walk across the room without becoming winded and needing supplemental oxygen. Every day was an endurance event for her. I wanted to highlight the fact that she was fighting every day to run her race, and honor how strong she was.

I called her to tell her about my race and that I was dedicating it to her. I was surprised by how touched she was to hear me tell her that. I then told her it was for charity and the organization was supporting research for Pulmonary Hypertension Disorder (PHD). Something I had never heard of.

Imagine my surprise when she responded "That's what I have!" I had had no idea that PHD was her specific diagnosis. Clearly, I was supposed to be in this race. When training would get tough, remembering that I was doing it for charity and for people who could not swim or bike or run that far, stopped me from complaining about the pain, or the training times, or the workload. I was grateful for the chance to try to do it.

Putting My Faith on the Starting Line

Race Day, June 2014: The air was crisp in Austria that morning. My friend and Academy classmate, Matt, dropped me off as close to the starting point of the Ironman race as possible. I had never swum 2.4 miles in open water, never biked 112 miles all at once, or run a marathon after being on a bike that long. I really had no idea if I could do this, but for some reason...the Lord had led me there. At least my spirit was sure of it, because my flesh was still having tantrums and wondering IF we could do this and not die.

Note: The flesh doesn't like walking in faith. It can't see or touch the things the spirit can and it makes the body uncomfortable. However, at this point I was more proficient at overcoming the resistance in my flesh. I had experienced the victory and spiritual growth of all that God had asked me to do so far to get to the race.

Technique: To calm my nerves I sing songs of praise in my heart.

As I walked to drop off my equipment I looked up to the sky. There was one cloud in the sky that morning and out of it beamed a small arc of a rainbow. My heart lit up.

When I see a rainbow, it reminds me of the promises of God. I began to smile and sing stronger in my heart. I looked up again and the rainbow was now a larger arc starting from the cloud and going all the way into the lake where I would swim 2.4 miles in open water.

The mass swim start included more than 900 athletes for the first wave and was easily my biggest fear that day. Swimming was my weakest element, where I had the least amount of experience. The rainbow gave me confidence that it was going to be ok. God was with me.

I dropped my things off, put my wet suit on and made my way down to the race start on the lake. As I crossed over the timing mat threshold, dividing competitors from non-competitors, identifying me as an athlete stepping up to the line of the race I had been called to run, I looked over to my right and standing there was a man of God.

He was a tall Austrian man with blazing clear blue eyes, dressed in a plain brown clerical robe with a simple cross necklace. He was smiling gently at me and I wanted to give him a big hug, but I restrained myself. Tears welled in my eyes as I felt further confirmation that I was in the right place. Another measure of confidence poured into my body and spirit.

Minutes before the race started my nerves began to scream their last moments of protest at the utterly ridiculous idea that we could do this. The priest began walking amongst the athletes, shaking hands and offering encouragement. As he passed right by me, I reached out and hugged him for comfort.

As I stepped back, this man of God, towering over me, smiled. He placed his hands on both of my shoulders, squared me up, looked into my eyes and said "Alles ist gut" Which means "Everything is good" My heart strengthened and with that, it was time to go.

The gun went off and I jumped into the thrashing of hundreds of athletes beginning to run their race.

Now, even though I was certain I was where I was supposed to be, I was still not that great a swimmer. I was giving that swim everything I had, but I could not keep on course. Each time I looked up, I was veering off 45 degrees one way or the other. The anxiety rose inside of me as I experienced the chaotic thrash of my first mass swim start. My body hit the panic button.

I began to pray. "Lord, I need help. I can't keep straight and this is making me have to swim farther to get back on course." My mind was telling me I could not afford to swim much further than 2.4 miles and finish the swim in the allotted time.

I said my prayer, kept doing my best, and waited for God in my heart and mind. I set my eyes on the horizon, which at this point was to finish the swim. My mind held fast that God provides for all our needs (Phil 4:19), I kept doing my best, and soon help arrived.

Another swimmer who was at my pace pulled up beside me. He then remained consistently at my speed (unusual), but could stay on course. This allowed me to use him as a guide to keep straight with every breath on my right. He stayed with me all the way out to the turnaround point and back towards the shore.

I came out of the water and looked at the clock. One hour and thirty-one minutes. Well within the cutoff time of 2hrs and 20mins. My heart soared and I came out of that water like I had won the race. And I had won the first race. My race. What I had overcome in self-doubt and learned in skill to get to that point were nothing short of miraculous for me and healing on a multitude of levels in my body, mind and spirit.

Next up, the bike challenge.

I spent a lot of time praying on that bike. First, I expressed gratitude that I was no longer in the water! I prayed for guidance about when to brake or slow down, how to pace myself and the regular request for God to renew my legs.

This was a two-loop course. I came around the first loop in about 3 hours. Memory recall; the week prior I had raced in Ironman70.3 Aarhus and my bike time for that same distance was 3 hours and 29 mins. I was faster this week. But now I had to do 56 miles again AND run a marathon. Did I have what it took to do another loop at the same speed?

A fire ignited in my spirit and I refused to slow down. I would do it again. Coming around the turn to start the second loop of the bike, I used the doubters in my life as motivation. I could see all their faces and how much they would enjoy being right if I couldn't make it. I couldn't let that happen out of respect for God. At the time, I didn't understand all the reasons He brought me there, but I was going to give it all I had out of respect for Him, like a kid wanting to make their parents proud.

I came off the bike with a time of 6 hours and 2 minutes. I completed the second loop at the same speed. High five!... and now for the marathon. This was my comfort zone, because I cannot get kicked in the head, drown, or crash my bike (and I had seen a few that day), the worst that would happen is that I could pass out on the side of the road (which, I also ended up seeing that day).

Technique: Here is a favorite scripture I use for when I see those things and fear tries to enter my mind:

"A thousand may fall at your side, and ten thousand at your right hand; But it shall not come near you."
—Psalm 91:7

As I raced that day, the long endurance course burned into my body. Every time I wanted to quit, I reached up to God for more strength. I had no idea what I was doing there, but I kept leaning on Him for strength and guidance to finish. As I pounded out mile after mile of the marathon, there was less and less of me carrying myself with my own strength, and more and more of God carrying me to the finish line. On my own, I was emotionally weak and defeated. But as my body weakened, my spirit quickened, strengthened, and began to push my body forward with the scripture:

"I can do all things through Christ who strengthens me"
—Philippians 4:13

Lessons Learned

What I didn't know when I signed up, is that once I started to go beyond ten hours of continuous racing, my metabolism would begin to burn calories from places in my body it had not in years. The pulsing drive of the race demands drove into my muscle and joints. Waves of emotions began to release throughout my body.

In the last 15 miles of Ironman Austria, sadness overcame me. The consistent burn of the race was disintegrating the strongholds where my body had trapped past trauma. A layer of emotions that kept me weighted down in life began to dissolve. Healing coursed through my veins as the sorrow emptied.

My prayer from the end of 2013, where I had asked God to help me with my sorrow, was being answered. My body was able to let go of some of the pain it carried, a wall came down and God's presence was able to draw closer to me as we crossed the finish line together and for the first time, I became an Ironman finisher.

The first year I competed, I completed 2 half and 2 full Ironman races. The point results of that first year put me on the silver Ironman All World Athlete list (top 5% of my age group around the world). That achievement shocked me. I had no idea I was capable of accomplishing something like that. I would have not competed that year at all without God's prompting. I would not have finished without His strength and encouragement pulling me through

Note: The human body experiences another type of healing from the effects of processing negative thoughts and emotions during movement. Cognitive therapy and changing your words are essential as well, but not all that is needed. If you have been speaking destructive words over your body for years, you have altered its structure. Also, decades of poor eating and listening to depressive things changes you in ways that are deeply ingrained in your system. It is not enough to just say things, you must also process old and new thoughts while the body is in motion and sometimes go to great lengths physically to heal the mind and spirit. This is why you will often see people who go through a tragedy, but then DO a hard thing, come out healed on the other side.

Including that experience, I have now completed 10 Ironman's and 5 half Ironman distances. The races are something God uses to heal my body, mind, and spirit and where I practice being dependent on Him for guidance and strength. God uses the physical training and racing to help discipline my flesh. I must remain dependent on Him for training and to finish.

The experiences are faith builders. On the course, I have moments of clarity where I am alone with Him. His presence fills me with peace, healing, closure, joy, beauty, and hope.

Note: I am not saying you need to do an Ironman to get closer to God. However, if you are not feeling challenged, either physically, mentally or spiritually, to go beyond your personal abilities, it is unlikely that you are exercising your faith. Don't concern yourself with how big the goal is. Start by just pushing yourself to feel a little bit of discomfort as you go beyond what you know you can do. This can be as simple as having the courage to go speak to someone you know you are supposed to speak to.

Learning about yourself is a lifelong process. Humans are complicated beings with many layers and aspects. Even after spending years on my own personal growth, I still discover things about myself I can't believe I missed. Therefore, without an intentional practice of discovering how God designed you, it will be difficult to get better at living more peaceful and moving on to experiencing even more of what God has in store for you to do.

Learning about how God made you and developing a relationship of trust with God is critical for optimal operation in this fallen world. You can get places by flying erratically, but it will not be pleasant, or efficient and will likely be more hazardous for yourself and others.

You can let your mind and emotions oscillate from high to low, positive to negative and let your body lead more than it should, but the days will not be as productive or enjoyable as when you operate from a place of peace. It will also be slow-going getting to your next destination in life. Speaking of which, where are you going?

Chapter 3
Before you take off...
Where are you going?

Keep Your Destination on the Horizon

Even with the best aircraft, if you don't know where you are going, you will never get there. As a life coach and personal trainer, I evaluate current conditions of my clients and then build a strategy to get them where they want to be. For physical training, the goals are easy to tie to actual numbers or events.

What about the spirit and the mind? How do you want those to develop over time? It is also possible to devise goals for your spiritual and mental growth. It is necessary to understand their maintenance needs to keep progressing towards your intended destination.

For example, 20 years from now what do you want your relationships to look like? An active and thriving connection with family and friends is vital to our overall health. The positive community of people you build for yourself will keep your heart rejuvenated and even affect your physical wellbeing.

Every day we need to monitor our gauges to know how effective our systems are operating and to keep us on track to our destination. When conflict arises in a relationship, if peace is always your goal, your horizon, then you have a solid point that you are trying to navigate it to through any turmoil.

How do we decide where we are going? Well, from the time you were formed there has been a divine creator with a plan for you (Psalm: 13-18). The first focus in this book is beginning to read the Bible to know God better so you can hear Him, and then learning to fly in a more consistent state of peace with Him. The increased harmony and trust with God allows you to open up to the bigger things in life that God has planned for you.

**"For I know the plans I have for you,"
declares the Lord, "plans to prosper you
and not to harm you, plans to give you hope
and a future."**
—Jeremiah 29:11

Technique: More often people I meet have a sense of something they are supposed to do. Their tasks are often not big, but get put to the side for long periods of time. Much like the direction I was given to teach exercises classes, these can seem like random projects. However, these tasks can lead to the next piece of your journey with God: an opportunity to grow, meeting a new person or the beginning of a new phase in life. Write out at least one task you KNOW you are supposed to be doing in your life right now:

1.

Note: The sooner you learn to listen and do the things you know you are supposed to do, the quicker you will be able to piece together information and develop a deeper understanding of your purpose.

Do not worry about what the actual job or task is at hand. If you know it is what God wants you to do, then go with it. You never know what bigger thing it is linked to. Until you begin making God's list your list, you are not going to get where you are supposed to be and you won't fully develop who you were meant to be.

Recalibrate and Realign Your Instruments

Before each flight, pilots will align their navigation (nav) equipment. This equipment is designed to read nav aides around the world that emit information to aide pilots through their mission. Before each flight we cross-check that we have the right nav aides dialed in.

Then we verify our known starting position with what the gauge in our cockpit should read from the nav aide. We align our instruments before each flight, cross-check what nav aide we are currently following is dialed in correctly, and identify which nav aides we will need as we move forward. If the instruments do not align correctly, they will need to be recalibrated.

As Christians, it is important to make sure our values are aligned with the Word of God and that we are following the right nav aides He has given us. How we incorporate incoming information from our environment is important. We need to make sure we are following the things God wants us to follow, and not what the world distracts us with.

Caution: We can be the receptors of harsh words or hurtful actions. Those can become faulty data in our navigation system. They appear in our lives as repeating loops of the same issues. Locating the faulty circuit is more easily done when we have experienced what flying peacefully forward is.

An example of a faulty wiring might begin as unforgiveness towards one person. Slowly over time it spreads through our entire spirit and begins to affect the accuracy of our navigation system. At first, it might not be noticeable. However, ten or twenty years of not forgiving can completely change your course in life and who you are.

Unforgiveness often enters into our hearts and minds after being hurt. What starts as a small faulty wire sparks anger, bitterness, and resentment over time. It can then lead you to a different place than you were meant be. Unforgiveness can cause us to take a powerful course deviation in our journey. Often overlooked due to our hurt or anger, we allow our jet to fly with it affecting our systems and decision making.

Caution: If you do not forgive others, you will be tormented until you do:

"...'You wicked servant! I forgave you all that debt because you begged me. Should you not also have had compassion on your fellow servant, just as I had pity on you?' And his master was angry, and delivered him to the torturers until he should pay all that was due to him. So My heavenly Father also will do to you if each of you, from his heart, does not forgive his brother his trespasses."
—Matt 18:32-35

***Warning**: Read that last sentence carefully. Not only will God not forgive you until you forgive others, but you will also be tortured until you do forgive. A quick look around society reveals the effects of unforgiveness in people. It affects health and wellness in addition to attitude and the ability to be kind and loving. The most destructive cases of unforgiveness I have seen are those who cannot forgive themselves. The pain of their own lack of forgiveness turns into harshness and spreads to those around them.

Procedure for working on Forgiveness towards others: **"And be kind to one another, tenderhearted, forgiving one another, even as God in Christ forgave you"**

—Ephesians 4:32.

Technique: I have found that repeating scripture out loud during physical movement is very powerful. My mind meditates better in motion than when I'm still. Speaking God's Word while running allows me to meditate on it. Then, I am hearing it as it becomes planted in my heart.

Aim to Do Better

As a pilot you always strive to become better. Athletes also do not train to maintain, they work to get stronger, faster and master their discipline. Merely showing up to train brings little reward. You must have a vision, a goal or a horizon that you are aiming for. Otherwise, you become lack luster in your efforts and it becomes a waste of time rather than bringing value to your life. As Christian's, we also need to be accountable to what we have been created for.

Just maintaining what you have is a deceptive goal. The body needs variety in movement to keep from overtraining certain muscles and letting others atrophy, causing a potential for injury. Your spirit also needs to be challenged so it thrives. Purposefully grow closer to God and see how it effects your spirit in positive ways.

Be mindful that every day you are practicing something. As the comedian, Jerry Seinfeld once said "even doing nothing is doing something." Fast forward what lifestyle choices you make now for the next twenty years. What mental attitude will be more deeply ingrained in your brain? The mind needs challenges to keep active and healthy. Those thoughts are also affecting your spirit.

Technique: One of my favorite things to do is to recall happy memories with my friends and family. It strengthens my mind with positive emotions and my bond with the important people in my life.

Our spirits thrive in an active relationship with God leading us. We never reach perfection in this life. There is always more to learn and ways to grow. This makes life an adventure and not confined to one set destination on earth. The possibilities for our growth are limitless.

Keeping Your Destination on the Horizon When things Get Tough

How do you do that? My friend Stephanie posed this question to me after the Barcelona half Ironman in 2015. I was describing to her how much I wanted to quit during the swim. It was a rough race for me that year. I wasn't prepared for the difficult climb profile on the 56 mile bike course and the swim was challenging for me.

The dark Mediterranean waters tested my novice swimming ability. I was elbowed or kicked several times due to the low visibility of the swim. The waves were choppy and at times I would swallow salt water when I went for air. The current was strong, and it was a fight to stay on course. I would have to stop, reorient myself, cough out water from my lungs and fight to get back into position. I wanted to quit so badly...but I didn't. "How do you do that? How do you keep going when a part of you wants to quit?"

Technique: First, I make a decision that sets my horizon. In this case, once I signed up for the race, I decided that there were only two options: I would finish it or they would pull me off the course. Then I work backwards from the destination to my current position. For Ironman Barcelona, I set up a race training schedule around my life. The horizon becomes the focus point for daily decisions in my mind. It is set at the right priority level amongst my commitments and training fluctuates around the rest of my responsibilities.

The finish line of Barcelona IM70.3 became my horizon. Every time something got difficult or unpleasant during life or training, I mentally pictured my horizon; the finish line of the race. I imagined more and more details of the experience. I developed a connection with where I was and where I wanted to be.

The same is true with our spiritual lives. My ultimate destination is in heaven with Jesus. When things get tough, I raise my head to heaven and think of my home in the next life. It puts the battles of the day into perspective and gives me strength to keep going.

> **Procedure:** "Do not be anxious about anything, but in every situation, by prayer and petition, with thanksgiving, present your requests to God. And the peace of God, which transcends all understanding, will guard your hearts and your minds in Christ Jesus."
>
> —Philippians 4:6-7

Technique: Put your mind in neutral when things get tough. Think about things that have no emotional charge to them. Sometimes it is too difficult to put your mind in full positive mode and maintain it when you are stuck in negative thoughts or the seriousness of the situation is pressing hard on you.

During the swim portion of the Barcelona race I focused my mind on my form. For the swim, I isolated each movement and analyzed it. My arm reach, the pull, keeping my head down, sighting, breathing rhythm. I forced my brain to focus on refining all the mechanical movements.

I cannot always be positive, but I can put my mind in neutral, concentrating on task-orientated thoughts. I can turn on the comedy channel, listen to a new sermon by my favorite pastors, or go for a run with my music.

I have a list of techniques to get my mind changing direction. I give myself time to process difficult new developments in life, but I am cognizant of how long I am allowing myself to think about bad things, especially if I cannot change them.

Practicing gratefulness is a necessity, but it does not work in every situation to eradicate negative thoughts that are stuck in our minds. By removing negative thoughts first, you can be more successful at getting positive thoughts back into your cross-check.

Caution: Negative mental thought patterns become strengthened like muscles in our minds every time we think them. Conversely, when you do not ignite that negative memory muscle, they weaken. For a fascinating look at the neuroscience of how your thoughts produce chemicals in your body and affect your health, and how neuroplasticity works, check out "Who Switched off My Brain" by Dr. Caroline Leaf.

By using task-oriented lists when negative thoughts are hard to push out, I am able to stop the flow of negative energy into my body. I recalibrate myself by putting a neutral mission in front of me. I keep asking myself questions on everyday items to reorganize what I can get done. Anything to avoid the negative thought pattern. During emotional low points of a race, I focus on the intricacies of my form, when I need to eat next, and getting to the next distance marker.

Technique: Shiny Object! This is anything fun that I am planning to do in the near or distant future. Maybe it is getting together with friends I enjoy on Friday night. Maybe it is the athlete garden right after the finish line. It is a well-developed thought of something fun that I enjoy thinking about and can immediately use to bring joy into my heart. It can be as simple as talking with a friend or a day out on the water kayaking or a planned trip.

For the last several years I have been fortunate enough to have a trip planned in advance. Most recently, I traveled to Brazil to race and restore myself. In January I felt God leading me to sign up for the end of May race in Brazil.

The time between signing up and arriving in Brazil happened to coincide with a personally difficult time in my life. So, whenever I had a difficult day and the negativity around me tried to pull me under, I looked outside the situation, outside of my jet, and found my shiny object on the horizon...Jesus and I were going to Brazil!

I saw myself there, racing off the coast of Brazil all by myself and completely alone with my God. Restoring myself and strengthening my heart, I could make it through another difficult moment, no problem.

To summarize, the first part of staying on track to your destination is making a firm decision. Know where you are going and why. When things get tough, when negative thoughts are flying through your mind, put it in neutral. Finally, build yourself a shiny object in the near future. Have something you are looking forward to short-term to help you move forward in times of difficulty.

Incremental Progress

The difficult parts of races can be like difficult parts of life. Success is often the decision to keep redirecting my mind to a smaller, short-term goal and celebrating progress as it happens. I keep my cross-check of information going and form a better analysis of my entire situation.

I break up the race or day into smaller segments. In the swim, I focus on making it to the first buoy. I lock onto its coordinates and focus on making it there. I do not think about any other portion of the race. If my mind tries to draw me away to panic, I pull harder in the water, increase my stroke rate or push through another breathing sequence.

When the urge to quit overwhelms me, I think about my kids. I can't tell them I quit. That's not who I want to be for them, and I move forward another few strokes. I put my mind in neutral and start focusing on maintaining the best form I can. I look for neutral, task-oriented things I can accomplish.

When doubt creeps in, I remember how far I have come and refuse to quit. I set my mind firmly; either I finish this swim or they pull me out of the water. There are no other options. There is no time for debate because the clock is running. The jet is flying and life is moving along.

Once we orient ourselves to the plan God has for us, it is important to align our instruments for flight. Remember, things like unforgiveness in your heart can become faulty wiring in your system and alter your course in life. Regularly check your gauges, flight plan, and destination to make sure they line up with God's plan for you. Stay dedicated to your mission by remembering you have a purpose.

With a decision on where you are going next. It is time to start learning our daily flight procedures.

Chapter 4
Flight Basics

Pre & Post Flight Checks for Endurance

In flying, we have a set flow of operations. We start with the Pre-brief; this is where we talk about the mission for the day. Then we check weather and airfield updates, file our flight plan with the air traffic control agencies, and check our equipment. There is a checklist of items to accomplish before we arrive at the jet and another set of checks to turn everything on and begin to taxi out for take-off and fly our intended plan.

After the flight, you shut down in a particular sequence. The jet is then serviced and readied for the next flight or for storage, and you are off to the debrief. You evaluate where things went right, wrong and how they could go better next time. Areas for improvement are identified or it is decided you are ready to learn the next skill if you are still in training.

Life also has a rhythm, and the body loves routine. A regular sleep schedule and proper nutrition will bring on a better mood and help you sustain balance during difficult and stressful situations. The more rhythm and intention we build into our life, the smoother things operate.

We need to identify problems before they cause a catastrophe. We can learn from our mistakes and set our intentions to improve tomorrow. A morning routine paves the way to success.

Currently, there are many articles and books written about the link between people who get up early and those who achieve more in life. Plus, more and more studies are touting the benefits of regular early morning exercise, meditation, planning or journaling before engaging with the world. These habits build on each other and can make you a healthier, stronger individual.

Design a solid morning pre-flight checklist and then hold yourself accountable to it. Everyone works differently, so if that is a struggle, hire a coach or consult with friends to figure it out. I encourage you to work your way up to having a solid morning and evening routine.

In the evening, take a few minutes and include a daily debrief with yourself. Identify areas that could have gone smoother and think about how to fix them for the next day. What went right? What needs to go better? What could you change about your nutrition, sleep or exercise that would make you feel better?

Mentally check in on the relationships that are closest to you. Were you fully present with your loved ones at some point during the day? Have you fed your mind any knowledge or encouragement? What would bring you closer to peace in your spirit for tomorrow? Set a goal for the next day or week to do something better, write it down, and hold yourself to it. This will help build intention in your life. You can also download the worksheet, "Build your Daily Pre&Post flight checklist" at vitalitytactics.com

Technique: Once you make choices, implement them long enough to be able to evaluate their effects. One day of a new habit is not necessarily long enough to evaluate its success. Do not toss something out before you give it the chance to start working. I recommend at least 14 days to implement something before it can be assessed.

** Develop your Cross-check **

This is it right here. The one thing you <u>need in life</u> is a relationship with Jesus Christ. How you implement that one thing into your life is the make or break of successful flying. For pilots, it is called the cross-check. The primary technique that is going to make your life flow is a cross-check.

Maintaining situational awareness and making good decisions while flying requires a good cross-check. A cross-check is the continual scan of the instrument panel, listening to radios and being aware of the next several things that are about to occur. Everything from airspeed and engine RPM, to a GPS latitude and longitude read-out, and radio calls must be incorporated into the pilot's thought process to paint a picture of their situation.

The key to a good cross-check is not to fixate on any one instrument for too long. Airspeed and altitude are life, but don't get so focused on these two instruments that you don't realize your engine is on fire! This flight basic gets better with practice over time.

There are some common gauge read-outs that we all need to monitor: faith, relationships with family and friends, community involvement, physical exercise, nutrition, finances, work. As you learn to fly each day, monitor your instruments and learn what makes them operate at optimal levels.

Some easy gauges to talk about and adjust are nutrition and exercise. Learn what your body needs to maintain level flight. Is there a certain time of the day you are low on energy? Experiment with different foods, fasting, elimination of excess, and eating on a different schedule to try and find a better operating point.

Gauges such as your relationship status with others, are far more complex and require more time to study, learn and understand. However, they fuel a large part of joy and happiness when properly maintained.

The one thing you need is an active relationship with God. He will lead you when to work on all areas of your life. Scripture study alone will not cut it. You have to get out there and put your faith into practice. I can read about how to fly an airplane all day. However, until I get out there and begin to experience what I read about, I've never flown.

Note: A pilot is only as good as their cross-check. During challenging situations, the constant cycling through all the gauges gives Pilots the current health status of the aircraft and improves their ability to make informed decisions. Your consistent check-in with Jesus in your life will maintain the optimal level of flying for your body, mind and spirit.

Technique: Begin paying closer attention to your current conditions. Pick three gauges to read more often during the day and learn how to operate that system so it stays within the operational limits of "healthy". For example, check your energy levels throughout the day. Learn how different nutrition and timing of when you eat affects your body. Do certain fuel mixtures cause erratic readings versus a consistent flow of energy?

Processing Cross-check Information

Whenever you think about a situation or problem to the point you are worried or stressed, you have lingered on it too long. Say a prayer about it, give it to God and, **Keep your cross-check going** Look at the issue long enough to mindfully assess it, but keep moving your scan. By keeping your information collection going, you keep your life more peaceful. Focusing too much attention on one instrument can distract from other issues that need to be handled as well.

We can become consumed by one relationship, health issue, or incident. Meanwhile, another gauge starts to dip below its limit because we forget to handle a different responsibility. Now what was one problem, has generated two or three more because of a failed cross-check.

Note: Do not assign unnecessary meaning to incidents that occur in life. For example, when someone does not return your text, do not allow your mind to go down a negative list of why they did not. All you KNOW is that they did not return your text. There is no reason to go further with the thought in that moment. Avoid letting your mind fill in the blank with negativity, make a mental note, and continue with your cross-check.

Technique: Assume everyone is doing the best they can in life. This makes you happier as well. There will be times that I am tempted to be unimpressed with someone's best effort. That is when I remember I am sure I can find someone who is unimpressed with my best as well.

An Active Peace

Once in the air, straight and level flight requires constant adjustments to the flight controls. Maintaining peace requires a constant flow of adjustments in thoughts, attitude and choices. In today's world, it can be challenging to maintain peace on all fronts.

Even during times of smooth air, clear skies, and ideal conditions we are inundated with distractions, sensationalized news drama, and temptations pulling our spirit and flesh in all directions. There are constant attacks on our peace, making it difficult to enjoy for any length of time. Spiritual emptiness, mental fatigue, and physical exhaustion are the new norm. Then, if an actual tragedy befalls our life we are at serious risk of taking on long term battle damage.

We have been given the tools and ability to live with the **"peace that surpasses all understanding"** and that peace **"will guard *our* hearts and minds"** (Philippians 4:7) through all situations. We are capable of walking **"through the valley of the shadow of death"** while fearing no evil (Psalm 23:4). We can learn to focus or minds, minimize distractions, ignore unnecessary drama and maintain our peace.

How do I maintain my daily balance and inner peace when life gets tough and I find myself in a valley? Flying calmly through turbulent times requires mindfulness about what we allow ourselves to focus on and for how long. It requires an active maintenance of prioritization and keeping yourself focused.

Another key component to keeping your peace is perspective. When a situation is overwhelming or causing a substantial amount of turmoil in your life, look for a different viewpoint. Big changes in life usually produce a large amount of energy. Even negative energy can be used to turn future situations to better circumstances.

**"But they that wait upon the Lord shall renew their strength;
they shall mount up with wings as eagles..."**
—Isaiah 40:31

Storms can produce strong currents of air during their build up. Eagles take flight to hunt during this time. They know they are able to stay airborne on these powerful air currents without expending much energy by simply spreading their wings. They float on the energy of the storm just waiting for the right moment. Then, by a simple turn of their wings they change their flight angle, dive down and become more powerful and successful at catching their next meal.

Watch for the opportunities that can arise from the difficulties in life. Sometimes, God is clearing a path for something better. Other times it can be used as a set-up for something you would never have the opportunity for if the storm had not occurred. This will take an active management of your focus, maintenance of your priorities, commitment to goals and balancing your perspective.

Regular maintenance and Injury Prevention for the Body

Aircraft are regularly serviced and maintained to keep in the best operating condition. Aircraft maintainers perform daily maintenance tasks and investigate and repair any issues identified. Aircraft also have regularly scheduled overhauls at the depot where they go through extensive checks, repairs and upgrades. The depot maintenance is scheduled before parts are likely to fail.

In the human body I equate regular maintenance to maintaining core strength, a regular sleep schedule, and having a solid exercise and nutrition plan. Try to remain aware of any nutrition deficiencies or dependencies.

Experiment with eliminating certain foods to see how they affect your system. Our bodies change over time and you could have developed an intolerance to certain food. There should not by any food or supplement that you cannot go without for one day.

Have a balanced relationship with your food and do not let the desire of sustenance get out of check. Many of us are guilty of overdoing the caffeine. If you can't go without it for a day, try to eliminate the emotional dependency.

Note: When you physically train the body, be mindful of anything that feels "off." I tape, ice, elevate, stretch, or rest any muscle that I feel the slightest twinge in. I keep training, but I take preventive steps to stop small pains from turning into an actual injury.

Develop Your Core Strength

A strong physical core makes daily activity easier and prevents injury. Likewise, a firm set of core values and beliefs will allow decision making to be simplified. You will know how to handle unexpected problems easier if you have a set of boundaries that you will not violate. Practicing gratefulness in your mind is also a way to maintain and build spiritual strength.

In the mind and spirit, your ability to adhere to your core values when you make decisions display their strength within you. Regularly check on the health of your core values by evaluating your choices. If your daily choices begin to trend away from your self-identified core values, it is time to go in for a spiritual maintenance check to locate the issue. As with any issue, try to identify the problem when it is small and easy to repair. Anytime a gauge is even a little out of limits, get it checked.

Practicing gratefulness is essential to strengthening your spiritual core and your mind. When we have a consistent practice of noticing or mentioning things we are grateful for, it makes our baseline happiness and contentment higher. This also sets a default response in our minds when a negative situation occurs. Your mind is unlikely to get overwhelmed with negativity for very long when there is a regular practice of gratefulness in place.

Be mindful that even positive core values can turn you into something you are not if left unchecked and become unbalanced. For example, it is great to be positive and find things to be grateful for even in difficult situations. However, it can be done to a fault when it doesn't allow respect for another's pain or suffering. This is when positivity becomes insensitivity.

Caution: Practicing gratefulness when you are already depressed can be a difficult task. I often felt ashamed for being sad because I had so much to be grateful for...how could I be sad? The devil would use my shame to silence me and keep me from reaching out to others when I was hurting. Work on building your gratefulness practice in both good times and bad. However, if this technique does not work on a certain day, do not let the devil capitalize on it. Keep it in your arsenal, but do not overly depend on it or become too upset if it is ineffective some days.

Learn How to Love the Hard stuff

As an Ironman coach and personal trainer, I design workouts. I have been the receiver of multiple eye rolls and sad faces when I introduce the next exercise or present a training plan. I take it as a sign that we are getting ready to make some real progress as we go beyond a mental barrier. You will not grow as an athlete without pushing further and harder. This also applies to your Christian life. Pros do not show up to just maintain their current level; they are always looking to get better. Time and pressure make diamonds out of coal.

"No discipline seems pleasant at the time, but painful. Later on, however, it produces a harvest of righteousness and peace for those who have been trained by it."
—Hebrews 12:11 (NIV)

I remember my half Ironman race in Zell Am See, Austria in 2014. The conditions were brutal; the temperature dropped almost 15 degrees in one day and there was a torrential downpour for most of the bike course. I was frozen like a popsicle on the bike and I was very upset to be there. I began to pray and ask God for comfort and guidance. What I heard back in my heart was "If it does not challenge you, it does not change you." Over and over again it came to my heart. I pushed through and became stronger for it.

In the end, I was not happy about the experience and very disappointed in my time. In hindsight, I should have been grateful that I did not crash on the course. I saw several ambulances on the bike course that day. I threw what I call a Finisher's Fit (not pretty) all the way from the finish line to where we pick up our finishers t-shirt.

At the table, there were two young girls passing out t-shirts. When I stepped up to the table their faces lit up. They handed me a race program....and asked for my autograph. I was incredibly humbled. They were excited to see another finisher while I was busy beating myself up over the time. It was a reminder to be grateful and not let my mind focus on negativity.

Technique: Don't just show up to your day, challenge yourself to be something more than yesterday. Change your motivation for difficult tasks. Occasionally I get through another day of work, training and proper eating by remembering that my kids deserve my best. Other times it is out of respect for the body God gave me to house his spirit in while on this planet. Sometimes, it is so I can become more effective in helping others. No single thought, thing or ideal will work in every instant. If you find it difficult to be consistent for a repetitive task, find multiple motivational thoughts or mental pictures to rotate through in your mind during the work. Or go neutral. Focus on what you need to do and finish it.

Now, anytime my students or clients are suspect at what I require in their training, I tell them "if it does not challenge you, it does not change you." When we are getting towards the end of a workout and fatigue is high, I tell them this is where it really counts.

You build your endurance and get stronger at the end of your current limit. You have to learn how to push through when you're tired. Learn to like practicing during difficulties, it's what makes you great. Persevering through what is hard for you now, makes you stronger later.

Likewise, our faith cannot grow if we do not take on challenges of faith with God. One of my favorite scriptures about this is: **"But without faith it is impossible to please God..."** Hebrews 11:6. If you are not filling that regular tingle of reaching the current limit of your faith and God giving you more to grow, start to look and listen for those opportunities of growth in your spiritual strength.

Technique: Develop connections with other people to help you build accountability in areas that you struggle to maintain progress. This can be as simple as having a friend regularly ask you about your plans or as focused as hiring a coach to help you. You need a form of accountability.

Signing up for races has helped me with my workout accountability. If I pay money for an event, I will show up and plan to finish it. That works for me, it might for you as well. I have found the more I invest my time, mental energy or money into something, the more likely it is that I will finish it.

Increasing your systems knowledge will help you become a better pilot. Knowing your personal body, mind and spirit systems will help you maintain your peace. Imagine the benefits of understanding how to keep your mind and spirit peaceful and operating in a physical body that feels healthy. We are designed to operate from a place of peace, straight and level flight, on our way to our next destination, with all the fuel and navigation information we need.

Like any new skill, there are common mistakes that people make in their first attempts. In the next chapter we will identify the common daily flight mistakes. By being aware of them, you are less likely to make them as often or for as long.

Chapter 5
Common Mistakes

Learning a new skill takes time to master. In the beginning stages of change and development, you will make errors or not quite get it right. This is part of learning. It does not mean that you are not capable. It only indicates that you need more practice, additional instruction, technique refinement or study.

The initial reaction to realizing you have made a mistake is not pleasant. We all like things to be easy to accomplish and work quickly. We want a magic pill and an instant fix. That is not realistic most of the time.

As you implement change, you are going to have to learn to manage your emotions through setbacks and even complete disasters without letting it give you an excuse to quit. To make matters potentially worse, when we are in a depressive state it can be easy for the devil to launch an attack on you using a recent mishap in your life.

The enemy attacks and overly focuses you on the negative aspects of the mistake. Soon, the event is much larger in your mind and emotions than it needs to be. You may lose the ability to look at the mistake objectively and learn from it.

During change, make a commitment to not be overly reactive when things do not go well. Distance your ego from that harsh inner critic and look at the situation from an academic standpoint. You might need a day or two before you are able to let go of the negative emotions and use the analytical part of your mind.

However, realize that mistakes are also learning opportunities. Do not let them mentally pin you down into condemnation or allow it to become an excuse to abandon your efforts of change. You still have a mission in life. If you are still breathing, then you can still make progress.

As a professional life coach and athletic trainer, I would like to take you through the common mistakes I see as people implement new techniques. Over the years I have found when I speak to clients about the common error tendencies I see before they begin, they are more mindfully aware of difficulties they may encounter.

Then, they can either completely avoid the mistake or lessen the difficulty they would have experienced. This also helps minimize the negative emotional impact that mistakes can have. When we know someone else had the same difficulty we accept ourselves making it more easily.

Overcorrection

From far away, straight and level flight looks like a solid and smooth process. However, inside a jet, it is a continuous series of small corrections to maintain course. Large corrections in power and pitch usually lead to a domino effect of over-adjustments and erratic flight. Most corrections to stay on course are minor but never-ending. After you have set your next destination in life, it will take daily, and sometimes moment by moment, modifications to stay on course.

It takes time to adjust your hand-eye coordination to the way physical inputs affect your aircraft. In your personal life, it will take time to understand how your systems respond to the changes you implement. When you begin to course correct in your mind, body and spirit, go for daily, incremental, refining changes towards your goals. Check how they affect all your other gauges, relationships, finances, career, etc.

An example of a correction I made in life was when I decided that I was going to quit complaining. I heard a sermon where the pastor equated complaining to not being happy with what God had provided. That sounded terribly ungrateful to me. I was motivated enough to quit cold turkey.

As I went through the next day, I would begin a sentence and realize that it was sarcastic in a negative way or a complaint. I stopped what I was saying mid-sentence. For about three days I had nothing to say. I had no idea my speech had become so negative. Cynicism is rampant in our society today and it can alter your thoughts being consistently surrounded by it, if you are not mindful of how it affects you.

To support this modification, I made small, incremental changes to my everyday words, conversation topics and thoughts. I spoke about the weather a lot for those first few days. The current weather conditions and the forecast for the next day. I was surprised at what little neutral or positive conversation I had in my life.

From there I started asking people about their spouses, significant others, children, and pets. Next, I learned about people's hobbies and then their dreams. I kept becoming more curious about those around me and their positive thoughts I could find.

This change slowly led to learning about and caring more for the people around me. I gradually replaced criticism of the world to mindful interaction with the people in my life. I couldn't go from negative speech to spirit-filled, positivity overnight. However, I could talk about something neutral or be quiet. Then, as time progressed my new daily practice helped me find other topics that made my interactions with others more life giving for all involved.

Getting Task Saturated & Overwhelmed

In the airplane we sometimes get what we call "helmet fires." Also known as "getting behind the jet." This is when things are really busy. The radios are a constant chatter, checklists are being run and you are in a critical phase of flight such as landing. This means you are also close to the ground and there is very little room for error.

You must prioritize any problems and actions to keep the jet flying safely and in the right direction. It takes practice to learn how to assess your situation, recognize what is important, not get overly fixated on any one issue and keep the jet flying safely. There is no place or time for excess emotion. You must develop a faster cross-check to keep your situational awareness sharp and evaluate developing situations quickly. Delegate tasks where you can and learn how to differentiate when things can wait.

The key concept to realize here is that the jet is still flying forward even if you are not ready. There is no pause button while you catch up. Our lives can be the same. If you are not ready for the opportunities of the day, you can miss out. Who knows how long those penalty vectors will cost you.

A lost opportunity can set you back minutes, hours and even years. God gives us opportunities but that does not mean they will wait for you. Time does not stop. The world keeps turning. We all need time to rest and recover, but I encourage you to be ready for those windows of opportunity in life.

Technique: There are times when our lives become very busy. Avoid the need to talk about how busy you are and how crazy things are. Just deal with it. We all have the same 24 hours in a day. When I hear someone complaining about how busy they are I think, you can't be too busy if you have time to tell me about it. Get through heavily task-saturated parts of the day with focus and purpose. Be grateful you are vital. Try to get better for the next time you have to deal with the situation and enjoy what you can learn.

Caution: Do not complain. It steals your joy and makes you less effective. Only if you have a solution or want to design a solution to a problem, do you need to talk about negative occurrences. Otherwise, just get through the unpleasant moment. The less you talk about it, the easier it gets, and the moment passes faster than when you focus on how unpleasant it is.

Note: Do not confuse the expression of pain and suffering with complaining. There is a fine line between the two. If you find yourself repeating a painful story, ask yourself what your intentions are. Is it for understanding? Compassion to help you heal? Those can be healthy forms of communication. If you feel better after a conversation then you are moving forward.

However, if the recounting or expression of an event is leaving you feeling flat or worse off, consider your intentions before the conversation began. Remember, we strengthen negative things in our mind when we focus our thoughts and words on them. Consider if the topic is something you want more of in your life. If it is not, take it out of your conversations.

Getting Fixated on an issue and losing your Situational Awareness

When problems arise, it is important to keep your cross-check going. Focus on an engine malfunction too long and your airspeed can begin to bleed off unknowingly. This could put you into a serious emergency situation as the aircraft will lose lift and begin to fall from the sky. Likewise, do not overly focus on one life issue and fail to realize there are other things still going on that need your attention. Do not give yourself additional issues by becoming fixated on one.

Remember, the devil will use distraction in any way possible. We should try to problem-solve, but not to the point it causes us worry or anxiety. When you sense pressure rise on the inside, it is time to move on to another thought or task. Spending excessive time trying to solve problems or worrying about something will take you out of your faith and into fear. This will manifest more things you do not want by your focus on them.

After an initial assessment and some trouble shooting or problem-solving attempts, move your focus to something else. Check your other gauges before you come back to the one indicating an issue.

By moving your mind onto other things going on in your aircraft or life, you do a couple of things. First, you bring in other information. Are there any other gauges telling you something is off? Next, you find things that are going right. This is great news! Also, you build a more detailed picture of information for better problem-solving capability.

Another benefit to widening your aperture while you're having an issue, is keeping your mind from getting flooded with stress. Fear and anxiety shut down problem-solving capability in your mind. Learning to keep your cross-check moving will help you stay balanced during the phases of problem-solving. This keeps your mind sharp and your emotions from getting too much control over a situation.

Garbage in, Garbage out

We use this saying in relation to entering our navigation plan into the computers on board an aircraft. If you accidentally enter a wrong "garbage" number into the GPS, you are going to get some crazy directions back. Likewise, if you put garbage into your body, spirit or mind, then the same will come back out.

Pay attention to what music you listen to, what you read, watch on t.v. and who you surround yourself with. You are being influenced by your environment. This can also drive the need to recalibrate your instruments when they become affected with the consistent input of degraded information.

Recalibrating—Our gauges can be off sometimes. For example, we could have a bad emotional feeling about a situation. It is possible that the feeling comes from the fact that you are tired and not that something is wrong. If possible, delay important decisions until you are well-rested and clear-minded in the morning. If not possible, before you "feel" like you should take a certain action, it is important to cross-check it with the Word of God in your heart.

Poor nutrition going into your body is equivalent to negative mental thoughts going into your mind. Be strict with what you allow in. Pay attention to what you are putting into your body and subjecting your mind and spirit to. Remember: Junk in, junk out.

Doing the Right Thing for the Wrong Reasons

I challenge you to start to cross-check what you put on your schedule with what you feel the Holy Spirit is telling you to do. If you don't cross-check yourself and only go off what you "should" do or have "always" done, you will miss things and be in situations you should not. Developing that listening ear with God will help you make wiser decisions.

Procedure: **"Trust in the Lord with all your heart, and lean not on your own understanding; In all your ways acknowledge Him, and He shall direct your paths"**

—Proverbs 3:5-6

The procedure of checking with the Holy Spirit about whether we should or should not do something, also protects us from wearing ourselves out mentally and physically. If you always feel that you are doing things for "everyone else" and not being appreciated, then you are probably doing the right things for the wrong reasons.

Whereas humans are limited in their ability to appreciate and give back, whenever you do things for God, your perspective is different. The mission set you do it for is much larger and all encompassing. It is no longer just between you and an individual. When you have a wider aperture of the situation, you will find an endless supply of energy to keep going.

Procedure: **"And whatever you do, do it heartily, as to the Lord and not to men, knowing that from the Lord you will receive the reward of the inheritance; for you serve the Lord Christ"**

—Colossians 3:23-24

By dedicating all you do to God, you can protect yourself from becoming emotionally attached to the outcome. When we humbly admit that we do not know where the journey for another one is going and that we only have a part in it, we can let go of the need to control the outcome. We do not always get to know the reason why God has us do or not do a thing, but when we trust Him we protect ourselves and honor His divine sovereignty. So, before you do something because it's "the right thing" to do, ask God if it is something He wants you to do.

Note: Always cross-check with scripture. If you "hear" God telling you to do something that is against scripture, then you need to reevaluate what you think you are reading on your gauges. God will not violate His own word.

When Your Technique Needs Refining

The issue I find with most other self-help techniques is their focus on one aspect of a person. They focus on only your thoughts, and do not address how to handle trauma trapped in the body. Another might show you a great way to break physically from an addiction, but then never handle the spiritual aspect of recovery. You can heal your body and have a great relationship with God, but you must also "renew your mind" or you will find it leading you right back into trouble.

We make incremental progress and change in life as we apply different techniques. For example, a new workout program is great, but after 6 weeks to 6 months, you will need to change it up. It will no longer be as effective. It is tricky to recognize when a technique that was once helpful, really isn't doing much or worse, hindering you now.

This is why I use the cross-check theory of implementing change. You have to hold corrections long enough to effect change, evaluate and the technique may work for a very long time. However, be wise to when they are no longer effective. The only one thing that always "works" is having a relationship with Christ because it is living and dynamic when properly maintained.

I had to work daily to make my arsenal of scripture strong enough to get me out of situations. I developed a base-line relationship and understanding of God with these. However, if I never went beyond those first scriptures and only did the same thing every day, at some point the relationship would stagnate and wither. God has you on a continual growth path. There will be new things to learn and do as we mature.

By avoiding the common mistakes of overcorrection, getting task saturated or overly fixated, you can accelerate your progress in the beginning. Or at least by being aware of them, you can be more mindful of how you are focusing your attention. This will help you to be more aware of what you input into your system and how to monitor and evaluate what is working for you.

Hopefully, this will prevent emergency situations developing. However, in this life we are likely to encounter less than desirable conditions. In the next chapter we look at how to further prevent emergency situations and what to do when they occur.

Chapter 6
Emergency Procedures and Prevention

There are common aircraft emergencies all pilots are prepared to handle if they occur. The procedures for recovery out of a spin, engine fire, fuel leaks, etc. We always do what we can to avoid a bad situation in flying. However, in the event we find ourselves in an emergency situation, we have prepared ourselves by practicing known procedures and checklists.

Let me say that again. There are known procedures for emergencies, but you need to try to avoid getting into emergency situations so you do not need them! Know your notes, cautions and warnings. Know them about your body, mind, spirit, life, relationships, career, etc. With that being said, let's discuss prevention first.

Defense Strategy

Procedure: Elevate the Importance of your Relationship with God

Jesus said to him, **"You shall love the LORD your God with all your heart, with all your soul, and with all your mind."**

—Matt 22:37-40

It is essential to your well-being to put your relationship with God first. When God becomes the most important relationship to you, you are stronger, wiser and more resilient. One prime element a divine relationship provides that no other human relationship can is the fact that you can never lose God. He is always present and active in your life as long as you allow it. There is no person that can guarantee their presence with you every second of every day for the rest of your life.

Humans, even the ones who love us, can be unreliable. They change their minds, change their priorities, behave selfishly, have a bad day, or fail to show up. People sometimes decide to change who they are; they are entitled to do so. When you elevate any human relationship above the one with God, you become more vulnerable to spiritual emergencies.

What if your most trusted friend moves away? What if their life is cut short? If you lose the person who has become your #1 in life, you set yourself up for devastation. It could be unrecoverable depending on the depth of the dependency. In fact, it is in everyone's best interest that you have God first; being someone's everything all the time, would be too exhausting for anyone other than God.

Now, if you lose the second most important thing in your life, you can still lean on the first. This allows you to stay flying during turbulent conditions. Nothing in this temporary life will surpass the value of our final home with Jesus. Do not let anything cling to your heart so tightly that it weakens your sense of purpose in finishing the work for which you were created.

This tactic allows you to train and persevere during tough times on the way to your goal. When things break, businesses fail, or people walk away from you, you can be cognizant of the fact that you still have not lost everything. God is still with you! No one person, relationship or failure can take away your purpose.

Cross-check on loss: When loss of things occurs in life...ask yourself whether you still have your eternal salvation. Yes, you do. Does Jesus still love you? Yes. Then you have not lost the most important thing. Any other material object that has been broken or lost...Well, it wasn't going to go to heaven with you anyway. At some point you were going to say goodbye to it. A treasured relationship? If they are saved, you will see them again. Take comfort that they are in perfect peace with our Savior and you still have a mission to accomplish before you rejoin them.

Note: It is unwise to make any relationship, job, business, pet, etc., more important than your relationship with the divine. By His own words, He is a jealous God (Exodus 20:5). Idol worship can easily slip into our lives. Keep guard against it for your own protection and to keep a resilient spirit.

Know Your Enemy

The ultimate adversary in our life is the devil. For many years he attacked my self-worth while I let him. He ran the same offense on me for years until one day I realized I was doing nothing to stop it. Of course he used the same thing, it worked. I didn't develop an effective defense for my mind until I began reciting and internalizing the scriptures about who God said I was in Him. My impenetrable defense:

God says you:

- Are loved (1 John3:1)

- Are Chosen, Adopted, Accepted (Ephesians 1:4-6)

- Are Forgiven (Colossians 1:14)

- Are free from condemnation (Romans 8:1)

- Are Complete in Him (Colossians 1:14)

When I put God's Word against what the devil was telling me, I knew who was right.

Ask yourself: "What are the tactics that normally work against me?"

Technique: Start paying attention to what was going on in your head before you ended up in an undesirable mood. Then, deconstruct the thought process back to its ignitor. What situation, incident or initial thought spiraled out of control? The devil will keep using it as long as it is effective. Design an alternate thought path to take for the next time. Unless you design a different choice for your mind to make, the devil will keep pulling you down the same defeated one.

Don't Be Your Worst Enemy

Sometimes leading up to an emergency situation, there is a chain of events that starts off with one small mistake. This is called an "error chain." When I evaluated the times I was ending up in a depressive state, I often found the spiral started with a stalled negative thought about myself.

My mind locked onto a negative idea and I focused on it. Then the thought grabbed onto other things in the day and cast a web of negativity over anything it could. Even when a situation was neutral, my mind could somehow make it negative.

I became an expert at this, not realizing it was my mental practice. While introspection or looking for solutions to our problems is normal, it can go too far. When have you overdone it? When it starts producing anxiety and worry.

Only focus on mistakes long enough to try and understand how you got yourself into a situation. Perhaps by doing so you can prevent them from happening again. Learn from miscalculations and become wiser. Remember:

"If any of you lacks wisdom, let him ask of God, who gives to all liberally and without reproach, and it will be given to him. But let him ask in faith, with no doubting, for he who doubts is like a wave of the sea driven and tossed by the wind"
—James 1:5-6

Retrospection is also a great opportunity to try and remember if you heard the Holy Spirit trying to lead you a different way and if you listened. Keep your mind balanced in the assessment. This is not permission to overly criticize yourself about the negative thoughts or feelings. Again:

Procedure: **"Be anxious for nothing, but in everything by prayer and supplication, with thanksgiving, let your requests be made known to God."**

—Philippians 4:6

Technique: As soon as I recognize anxiety or worry bubbling up, I switch it to a prayer and ask God for what I need. I use simple prayers, "Lord, heal my mind" and repeat them over and over. This way, I am able to build a barrier from the other thoughts cycling through my mind. I recognize I have to push the power of positive or neutral thoughts to keep from stalling and breaking into a spin of negativity that I might not be able to recover from that day.

Caution: Negative thought patterns release chemicals (cortisol). High levels of cortisol sustained for hours can cause physical damage and actual pain. This is the setting in which addictive behaviors can develop. The body seeks to soothe the physical pain by either eating excessive amounts of comfort foods, drinking alcohol or any other potentially addictive behavior that can temporarily relieve physical pain.

Emergency Situations in the Mind

One of the worst situations you can find yourself in an aircraft is an uncontrolled spin. This is where the aircraft becomes unresponsive to the flight controls and is spinning out of control towards the ground. Our minds can feel much the same when they are flooded with intense emotions of a difficult situation or stuck in the replay of harmful thoughts. Finding a horizon, breaking the spin sequence, and navigating through the storm while staying on course to your destination is a skill that you can refine.

Before an aircraft breaks into a spin, there is normally a stall. This is when not enough air moves over the wing and lift is compromised. The aircraft experiences a buffet as the airflow is interrupted, and there is a distinctive choppy feeling as you fight the controls to pull back too far. The aircraft begins to sink and the flight controls become useless as the aircraft falls towards the ground out of control.

Healthy thoughts not properly flowing through our minds can cause a stall and put our spirit into a negative spiral. Our thoughts are a primary driver in our overall emotional state. There are outside stimuli that can give us a negative reaction. However, we can choose our follow-on perspective and how often we continue think about negative situations or focus on negative thoughts. But how do you recover from a spin once it starts?

First, I would like to present the **T-37 Boldface Procedure** for recovering out of a spin:

1. Throttles—Idle
2. Rudder & Ailerons—Neutral

3. Stick—Abruptly full aft and hold
4. Rudder—Abruptly full aft and hold full rudder opposite spin direction
5. Stick—Abruptly full forward one turn after applying rudder

6. Controls—Neutral After spinning stops, Recover from Dive

Notice that the first actions are neutralizing. They require the pilot to pull the power back (throttles-idle) and neutralize the flight controls (rudder & ailerons-neutral). The next three steps are abrupt, distinctive actions to snap the aircraft out of the spin. The last step is to neutralize the abrupt inputs, and recover the aircraft from a dive.

By snapping the aircraft controls opposite of the spin, it catches air on the wing, lift returns, and breaks the stall that rendered the controls ineffective. Now, in only a dive, the flight controls become effective again as air flows over the wing and creates lift. You can pull the controls back and recover the aircraft to straight and level flight.

Likewise, the mind has a similar procedure that can help snap it out of a downward spiral. **Mind Boldface Procedure** for recovering out of a spin:

1. Thoughts—Neutral
2. Breathing—Regulated
3. Body Tension—Released

4. Pray
   • "the Lord my God is with me wherever I go"
   • "they that wait upon the Lord shall renew their strength"
5. Physically move the body to a new activity or position

6. Break the Isolation

Note: You can use any prayer for step #4. This procedure requires that you have a pre-set list of neutral thoughts or encouraging scriptures to repeat and focus on. Have these options ready before any indications of a stall begin.

First, gain control of your physical self. This means you must neutralize your thoughts, emotions and calm your nerves. Begin to pray either out loud or quietly in your mind. Change locations to help clear your thinking. Engage in mindful, specific tasks to help neutral or positive thoughts flow over you, so you can catch the momentum you need to snap the negative thoughts out of your mind.

Lastly, break the isolation in your mind. You can be in a room full of people, but still feel alone. I spent years in isolation because the outside world thought everything looked perfect. No one thought to really connect to me and ask how I was doing. The intimidation factor of speaking to someone who appears all together, also kept others from reaching out. The assumptions were isolating.

To break isolation, speak to someone. It does not have to be about why you are upset. The goal here is to break the negative spin in your mind. Conversation is an excellent way to make the brain do something different. Focus your attention on asking the other person easy conversational questions. The weather, their family, etc. Your goal is to neutralize harmful thoughts. It can be done in person or over the phone.

Music can also help sync the mind. Be very careful what you choose to listen to. Praise and worship music is the best option. Happy, upbeat or neutral at a minimum. Try to avoid the lure to anything angry or sad. This heightens the issue in your mind and body, pulling your spirit with it.

The Body

There are sensations in your body that can alert you to an upcoming emergency. For example, a blood sugar crash can adversely affect your mood. Learn the warning signs. For me, it is irritability and a sudden urge to eat. I know I will become short tempered if the situation is not remedied soon. I identify the reason for the out-of-limits reading and then decide that until I can get some fuel to regulate the physiological need which is now starting to affect my emotions, I will avoid speaking with people.

Of course, I can ignore the indications. But if I don't handle the situation soon, I will find myself in a downward spiral and risk doing damage to the relationships in my life. I become easily irritated and my ability to remain patient and calm is degraded. I need to exit the situation quickly before I create a disaster. If I can't add fuel to my system before the spiral is out of control, I will initiate my boldface procedure: Eject! From social situation.

Memorize emergency procedures and scriptures for your unique life. What works for you will also change over time and circumstance. Begin to identify the things that put you into potential risk for developing into an emergency so they can be avoided.

As tired as we have all become in today's hectic life, fatigue often sets the stage for causing problems. I have found that sometimes when I think I'm sad, I am actually so tired I can feel it throughout my entire body. My boldface scripture for when I am tired in everyday life and/or when I race the full Ironman course is:

**"But those who wait on the Lord
Shall renew *their* strength;
They shall mount up with wings like eagles,
They shall run and not be weary,
They shall walk and not faint."**
—Isaiah 40:31

Watch out for Potentially Addictive Behavior Developing

When I have found addictive behavior start in my life, it is normally associated with unresolved pain. The wound in my mind or spirit hurt to such a degree or length of time that I began to feel pain physically. Prolonged discomfort in the body causes a physiological drive to self soothe. The body will do this in whatever way it can find. Eating, shopping, drinking, lust, gambling, the list of addictions goes on. The body triggers the mind to soothe its discomfort and does not care about the long term consequences.

The actual addiction is only part of the issue. The other part of the problem is the unresolved pain that is driving the body to look for relief. If we do not resolve the pain issue in a healthy manner we will then have two problems instead of one: the addiction and the root cause of the pain we were trying to escape. The body needs a healthy alternative to soothe itself once it becomes physically upset as a result of negative thinking or emotional pain.

For example, when negative thoughts or stress make someone physically agitated, drinking alcohol is a common way to calm nerves. However, this can create a dangerous loop. Alcohol is a depressant and this loop is a deceptive one.

Most people will experience an almost immediate relief of physical pain or mental frustration from the first glass of alcohol. The depressant effect is normally not felt until several drinks later and most often THE NEXT DAY. The following day is when we often feel awful, tired or sad.

Then, if you have an ongoing negative situation in your life, paired with a body that is still detoxing from a depressant, you are setting yourself up for wanting another hit of the initial good feeling the first glass of alcohol can give you. Rinse. Repeat.

Technique: Do not focus on how the first glass makes you feel. Remember how you feel the next day. There is nothing good for you after the first glass. *Nor the first if you are ready to accept that piece of information.

Techniques to self-soothe during anger, sadness, loneliness, emptiness, frustration, etc:

- Go for walk. If you need more power, go for a run or lift weights, do pushups

- Watch or listen to a comedian: Save your favorites on a Netflix list or podcast so they are ready to play

- Watch your favorite movie

- Read a book

- Diffuse Lavender (this can actually physically change your brain waves)

- Make a warm cup of coffee/tea

- Take a hot shower or bath

- Call a friend and have them talk about their day or something they love

Note: This book is not attempting to solve any seriously developed addictions, but warning to stay out of them and giving alternative solutions for handling physical pain caused by emotional and mental stress. If you have this book in your hand and can still focus long enough on the information to read it, you still have the ability to help yourself in some way. You may require additional help as well, but the addiction has not yet taken your mind completely. If you are suspicious you might be in danger of losing to an addiction, seek professional help immediately.

Spatial Disorientation

A dangerous condition that can happen to a pilot is known as spatial disorientation (spatial-D). Your body senses when you turn an aircraft right, left, climb, or descend. However, your internal gyroscope can be disrupted by visual effects. For example, a pilot that has spatial-D can feel that they are in a descending turn, when they are not.

The natural inclination is to correct back to straight and level flight from the "feelings" the jet is giving you. However, a cross-check of the instruments reveals that the aircraft is in straight and level flight. Pilots suffering from spatial-D feel the instruments are wrong and can put the aircraft into a dangerous situation. The pilot will have to fight against the sensations of the body and fly by the instruments. Some cases of spatial-D have been so significant that they caused the pilot to crash the airplane.

How do we relate this to our Christian lives? Living only by how you feel is dangerous. Emotions are useful, but must be cross-checked with other data. Emotions can and will fluctuate. You need a firm horizon to check them against. You can have peace, feel that you heard God, and a good cross-check with the Word of God will hopefully confirm that you are correct.

The key to staying out of emergency situations is to practice preventive techniques and be aware of what could put you in harm's way. By having a good defense and knowing your enemy, you become wiser. However, if you find yourself in "the valley of the shadow of death,"remember that:

"...they that wait upon the Lord shall renew their strength; they shall mount up with wings as eagles; they shall run, and not be weary; and they shall walk, and not faint"
—Isaiah 40:31

Not every day in this life will "feel" victorious. What happens when we experience an emergency and need to reevaluate our way to our next destination the Lord has put before us? We start the replan!

Chapter 7
The Plan Meets Reality

It's go time. You have your plan and see clearly what your next step with God is. You are trained-up and have all your supplies. What happens when the plan completely falls apart from the time you step out of the door? Does it mean you were wrong about what you heard? Maybe. It could also only be a minor setback and you just need to regroup and try again. Check scripture, check in with your spirit. Pray.

Aviation Weather: What are the conditions for today? Although a plan is necessary, you must adjust for actual conditions on the day of.

Even when you are on the right path and course, there will be setbacks. We operate in a fallen world and there is an enemy that creates obstacles. Pray. Keep to the plan you know God gave you, but realize there are times we are meant to work hard in this life. God will make sure you have what you need, but you fly with Him, not sitting idly by.

I used to get very upset when things didn't go as I planned. Then I realized that the chances of that happening 100% every day were next to zero. In fact, anyone can plan, but the real art is in the replan. As we often say in the Air Force, "No plan survives first contact with the enemy". When times become overly frustrating and I want to give up, I remember this scripture:

"And let us not become weary in doing good, for in due season we shall reap if we do not lose heart"
—Galatians 6:9

Remember, at the beginning of the day you have an initial plan. You take your known variables and make the best structure to meet your end result or goal. Do not develop too close of a relationship with the initial plan. It will meet the reality of the operational day and likely meet its end.

"For a just man falleth seven times, and riseth up again..."
—Proverbs 24:16

Aircraft break, aircrew get sick, and the list of delays can be endless. At the end of the day you look at the progress you made and replan to try and achieve closer to your goal the next day. Life is much the same way. You get sick, the car breaks down, you forget something at home. Things happen.

"But as for you, brethren, do not grow weary in doing good"
—2 Thessalonians 3:13

Keep pressing forward. The beauty is in the journey with God. Every time something goes off-track, keep an open mind, listen for correction and try to learn something. Practice this with your daily plans and adjust your timing towards your long-term goals and plans. You will make more progress some days than others.

We cannot normally see the entire picture of our life all at once from beginning to end. Therefore, it is important to remain humble to the fact you might have missed an important stop along the way and may need to back track or reroute.

What is the point in planning if it is highly likely to not go as planned? You need a starting point to begin your journey. You will be better prepared if you have an initial framework of what to expect. As Dwight D. Eisenhower once said "Plans are useless, but planning is indispensable"

Learn How to Bounce

In this life you will make mistakes and sometimes get thrown to the ground hard. Learn how to turn that energy into a bounce back up. Study how to keep moving forward after making an error. I used to think that happy, successful people just had it easy and that is why they were so content.

One of the things I did when I found myself depressed was I studied happy people. I was shocked to find that they did not always have perfect, easy lives. However, they made a choice to focus on the good and not to think about the bad so much.

I also learned that successful people often failed many times before they became successful. Even those born into money may have financial difficulties or family problems they must navigate around. On the flip-side, there were also people with "easy" lives that were miserable. It seemed to me, there was a choice about how you looked at what you had and processed it.

What these people all had in common was not luck, it was that they knew how to get back up, learn from their mistakes and keep moving forward. Not only forward, but they had the audacity to think it could get better than the awful thing that happened to them!

I had to accept that part of my sadness was likely my own fault. That hurt to realize. However, the good part about getting myself into that situation, I was the one who could learn how to get myself out. I turned what was initially a negative thought, into a source of power. I then had more control over my situation.

Caution: *Do not take this paragraph out of context and think it to mean that I am saying that my thoughts alone were what had gotten me into and kept me in a depressive state, or that by fixing my thoughts alone I could come out of it. Depression is a multi-faceted enemy and attacks all three of our parts differently. The physical body suffers from depression differently than the mind and spirit. What heals the mind, does not immediately correct what years of depression has done to the physical body. A spirit wounded by living with a depressed mind, will need time to heal. Years of depressive thoughts can also chemically and structurally change your brain.*

Simply changing your thoughts is not enough. Remember, there are three parts to all of us. A distressed spirit can pull the mind into sad thoughts. The mind then begins to generate negative activity that can heighten pain in the body. You must heal each in its unique way, or relapse is likely to occur.

Coming out of depression is a hard task. You must do the different work needed to repair your body, mind and spirit. Your gauges will need to be repaired, as well as the systems that they monitor. It takes commitment to a recovered, peaceful destination to make consistent progress. You have to believe that:

"with God, all things are possible"
—Matt 19:23-30

When you know why you keep pressing forward it will keep you strong. An aircraft fueled by a shaky set of beliefs will not last through difficult times. You will likely need more than one answer or reason to keep pushing forward, especially for longer periods of the same battle.

Note: I never got very far setting goals and planning for my own desires or what I logically thought I should be doing. When I plan with God as my primary guide, more energy flows through me, more peace inside of me, and I have what I need to go the distance for God and others.

Unusual Attitudes

In flight training, the instructor will have you close your eyes, they'll put the jet in an abnormal attitude then tell you to open your eyes and "Recover!" You have to use your instruments, the horizon and your decision-making ability to reset the jet to straight and level flight. This is done in order for you to practice developing your situational awareness with your instruments.

Sometimes you wake up in life and think "How the heck did I get in this place?" You find yourself in a job, a relationship or a task that feels wrong or is even outside of your core belief system. Through some decision chain you have made an error and are now upside down, flying erratically and have no idea where you're actually going. You may unexpectedly find yourself, once again, in darkness.

To recover the aircraft, just like getting back on track in life, immediately get back to straight and level flying. Engage in neutral thoughts and activities and stop doing anything that is against your core values. It might be painful to stop abruptly, but do not waste time with things that go against your integrity or are negative in any way.

"Do what is good and run from evil so that you may live! Then the LORD God of Heaven's Armies will be your helper, just as you have claimed."
—Amos 5:14-15

Do not waste time trying to figure out how you got there while you are still in the midst of the unusual attitude. Talk about how you got in the situation later so you can learn from it. But first, work on restabilizing the current situation back within normal operating limits and get back to flying to your intended goal.

Rewiring

Wherever you are when this book finds you, I hope it helps you to begin rewiring your mind. Our thoughts are connected to how we feel in our spirit and our bodies. The circuit can flow both ways. Our thoughts can affect our spirts and bodies, but also our bodies and spirit can affect our minds. The goal is to be spirit-led. Finding and ridding yourself of faulty, hurtful or defective thinking can be the start of finding more peace in your life. As we discipline our flesh and heal the body, we will find more peace in our minds.

Procedure: **"Do not conform to the pattern of this world, but be transformed by the renewing of your mind. Then you will be able to test and approve what God's will is—his good, pleasing and perfect will."**

—Romans 12:2

It takes a lot of mental effort to change your thought patterns. Thoughts that are hard-wired and stuck on repeat become strongholds in our minds. The neuroscience of it is fascinating.

Dr. Caroline Leaf, a cognitive neuroscientist, describes memories as tree branch-like structures in our mind. Each time you have the thought, the branches wave and release chemicals. Happy chemicals are released when recalling good memories and harmful chemicals such as cortisol are released when recalling bad memories.

The more often you move those branches when you think those thoughts, the stronger the branches get. The less you recall the thought or memory, the weaker the branches grow. The memory can die.

Technique #1: Rebuild your mental structure with a new commitment or project. One that requires a lot of focus and effort. Learning something new is incredibly good for your brain and has anti-aging effects. If you can tie it to another goal or something else that is important to you in life, even better. For example, I wanted to be a triathlete, but I didn't know how to swim. The desire to be an Ironman helped to fuel my dedication in the pool.

Being in the pool and trying to learn how to swim forced me to think about one thing, breathing. Since my breathing was restricted, I consistently panicked about not having enough air, and ta-dah! I was not thinking about anything else other than how to survive in the pool. My mind took a break of at least 30 minutes from negativity as I tried to learn how to swim each day. Those 30 minutes afforded my mind time to heal and build a healthy, neutral space of activity for it to go.

I have always wanted to learn how to play the piano, so I signed up for lessons. Even that small 30-minute window gave my brain a break from negative thoughts and helped steer me away from destructive behavior.

In another difficult part of my life, I took a hot yoga class every day for 5 days straight. For an hour and a half, I was in a 100 degree room with 85% humidity and a teacher rhythmically directing my mind to move my body in certain ways. Even though I was in shape when I took the class, it was a different form of exercise and I was exhausted afterwards.

During the class all I could think about was what the teacher was saying. She guided my mind. The new sequence of challenging movements paired with an instructor that my mind had to follow, allowed peace for my spirit during a difficult time.

Accountability and an investment will also increase success when rewiring your mind into a more peaceful state. Decide that if you are going to spend x amount of money or devote y amount of time, you will achieve a defined end result. Set definable goals such as: I will be able to play this song on the piano. I will learn how to swim and finish an Ironman. I will make it to yoga class 5 days in a row.

Technique #2: Teaching a community class or volunteering to lead a community project will also help expose your brain to responsibility and accountability. There are endless ways to help in this world. Finding a cause that you have a passion for and donating your time or talent REGULARLY, will aide in transforming your heart and mind.

Make a short-term commitment if you can't commit to something big YET. Rewiring your old, destructive thought patterns requires work. A goal that is tied to a bigger cause will help you have the support structure you need to begin rebuilding your mind to an improved state of peace. A commitment to show up and do something for others will help your spirit and mind become stronger as you serve others.

Recovery

How you recover the mind, body and spirit each day matters. The cumulative effects of basic self-care are essential, but so is the mindset during recovery from difficult situations. As an Ironman athlete, I take my post-training and post-race recovery very seriously. As a result, I recover quicker than most and do not suffer unnecessarily.

The mindset you choose when you recover from a difficult life situation is critical to how you develop emotionally over time. Take notice of how you frame your life stories. As time passes, pay attention to how you change the details. Especially the difficult ones. Do they become more negative, neutral, or show understanding and growth? Keep the words of your good memories vibrant and with as much depth as you can remember.

As we experience this life our spirit also evolves and changes. As Christians our intention and path should be to become more Christ-like. **"But we all, with unveiled face, beholding as in a mirror the glory of the Lord, are being transformed into the same image from glory to glory, just as by the Spirit of the Lord."** (2 Cor 3:18) Stay intentional in the recovery process so that you are rejuvenated by your journey instead of feeling further broken-down. It is a mindset and a choice to keep moving forward and improving.

Sometimes we get off track. Never worry that God cannot find you. Like the world's best GPS, He can reroute you in an instant. Learning how to replan, bounce back and rewire a better structure in our hearts, mind and body is a continuous process. I urge you to continue this refining without ceasing. Choosing not to adjust and follow guidance has far-reaching consequences for yourself and others.

I prayed, and Nothing's Happening

There are long journeys to some destinations. These missions try your patience and fortitude, but can be faith builders with the right perspective. What happens when you have prayed, have been standing in your faith, and nothing seems to be happening? The temptation to give up begins to grow. Our vision to the destination gets clouded by obstacles or strongholds in our mind.

As you dig deeper and keep going, remember the bigger picture of things to keep perspective. Reassess your current position in relation to your destination. Maybe you have made more progress than you realize. Go through your cross-check of all your life instruments and look for ways to be more effective in your day.

Are there scriptures you are standing on? Stand firm. Pray, seek God and keep running your race. Remain humble and always open to the idea, you could be just slightly off, so keep the communication with God flowing for any course correction.

In our quick-fix society, we are tempted to try to take short cuts or look for simple answers. The easy way is often the longer road while the hard way...is the shorter road. Incremental adjustments build strong foundations, but they take time.

The daily grind changes you in microscopic ways that are often imperceptible in a two to three-day sample. We want to go to the gym for three days and look great. Try six months of hard work before you can see a noticeable difference in your body.

Noticeable spiritual changes can also be difficult to recognize until you look back six months to a year. Keep pressing forward, ask for more strength and wisdom, keep your ears open, and do not grow weary in doing good. Just because you can't see the progress now, doesn't mean it isn't happening.

When things start to become difficult, it can be an opportunity to build your strength. It is also a great setting for going deeper into your relationship with God. If nothing ever gets difficult, then you can easily be fooled into believing that you do not need God. You get further away from the natural dependence that we are created to have with Him.

Recover setbacks and replan with added emphasis on lessons learned along the way. By keeping your eternal destination on the horizon, your mind will see situations in relation to God's plan and help you keep a balanced perspective. Your cross-check becomes more informed and you can #RunYourRace even better.

Chapter 8
#RunYourRace

I have two specialties as a coach. 1) Teaching people how to get back up and 2) Delivering the truth of situations in a direct manner for clarity. Each time a person comes into my life and a coaching conversation develops, my heart smiles. I know that if we cross paths in that setting, it usually means it's time for you to get real and hear something new to help you.

I greatly enjoy sharing those moments in time with someone. The words that need to be delivered to that person ring clearly in my heart. In a powerful moment I feel the Holy Spirit use me for His purpose.

This is also where I have learned how to teach someone to keep going when life gets tough. How God can use the right words to reorient their vision and adjust their course. I have seen how realignment on the right navigation aids can help someone keep going when a moment ago it seemed impossible.

After ten full Ironman's I have also come up with and tested some solid strategies for persevering. I have spent over 1,757 miles racing around the world discovering what works and what doesn't to keep going. It takes spiritual leadership of your mind and body to arrive at a pre-determined destination. You have to find what sparks your heart to keep the internal energy flowing in your physical being.

Teaching someone else how to keep going requires asking the right questions. Inspiring a person to dig down and find a little bit more necessitates me to help them find the core of what they are made of. You need more than one reason to answer your why's when life puts pressure on you for extended periods of time.

At the beginning of every race, this question still presents itself to me: "What are you doing here?" It is the same question that the devil brings up every time he is trying to disrupt my journey. You have to find the answers that strike your spirit when the obstacles show up.

The devil is persistent. There will never come a time when he will quit trying to disrupt your life, or tarnish and dilute the brilliant person God created you to be. If the devil can make you less effective he has won something.

He may not win your soul, but if he can make your life a mediocre existence compared to what it could have been, he'll take that as a win as well. I hate that vision and find it motivating at times to dig deeper. Remember in the intro how I mentioned that the devil would come back around and use the same offense tactics on me again?

In 2013, before asking to be closer to God, before being told to go teach exercises classes, and then going on to run my first Ironman race, I had to win an important battle within myself first.

That year the gloomy German winter surrounded my bedroom and pressed in on me as I laid on the floor. My emotional pain was now causing me physical pain. I couldn't get up. I couldn't move. The effort it took to breathe seemed like too much. The devil had me pinned down mentally...again. The eerie familiarity of the situation haunted me.

Darkness encircled my body. My personal life and family were in disarray. There was no peace in our home. The pain of a dying marriage, shame, and the feeling of being a failure tightened like straps around my body as my breathing shallowed. The only prayer

I could form was "Lord, help me find my peace again"

In that shadowy moment the devil reached for one of his old favorites, the doubt card; *"How can God exist if you are in such pain. What kind of God will let someone they love suffer like this?"*

I had no reaction, and he reached for another popular winner: *"You, a Christian...depressed? I thought you had victory...peace...joy. You can't even get up."*

My thoughts went to the scriptures he was speaking to. The Bible is full of references about having peace, victory and joy available to us in Christ. I hate it when the devil uses them against me. He's attacking my spirit and my mind...Why am I in this deep state of sadness, lacking even the strength to get up?

Well, let's break this down in my mind since I can't get off the floor. How did I end up in this state? One possibility is that by living in this fallen world, I am a casualty of the spiritual war that surrounds us. You can be a trained soldier, but the enemy can still take you out with second and third orders effects of the ongoing spiritual conflict that surrounds us all.

I could be experiencing someone else not being where they were supposed to be or not doing what they were called to do. Perhaps someone has misused their free will and either purposely or negligently hurt someone...who is now hurting me.

If so, God can remedy anything as it plays out because **"We know that all things work together for the good of those who love God: those who are called according to His purpose"** Romans 8:28. Either way, my current state in a single moment of time does not prove or disprove the existence of God or His Word. Nor does it mean I am not going to have a victory any minute now...

The second possibility is that I am in this situation due to my own rebellion. That one burns a bit to confess. However, if I am perfectly honest with myself, I am not 100% obedient, 100% of the time. Sometimes, I do not listen.

"Woe to the rebellious children," says the Lord, Who take counsel, but not of Me, And who devise plans, but not of My Spirit, That they may add sin to sin;"
—Isaiah 30:1

So, it's quite possible that I got myself into this situation because I chose not to listen. It's a good thing I know my way out of that predicament since I have found myself here one time or a hundred over the years. Repent. Ask for and receive Forgiveness. Request Help.

But the devil is again quick on the doubt *"What kind of a God would help a person like you? You are worthless and rebellious by your own words. Abandoned by family, friends…at some point every one leaves you."*

My heart erupts back with **"…I will never leave you nor forsake you"** (Hebrews 13:5). I have made it a policy not to argue with God's Word. I accept it as fact whether I can "Feel" it or not. I take God's Word as truth. And so, I also know that I am not worthless because in God's eyes I am:

- A child of God (John 1:12, Romans 8:16)
- Loved (1 John 3:1)
- Forgiven (Colossians 1:14)
- Redeemed from the curse of the law (Galatians 3:13)
- Free from condemnation (Romans 8:1)
- A new creation (2 Corinthians 5:17)
- Chosen, Adopted, Accepted (Ephesians 1:4-6)
- Given access to God (Ephesians 2:18)

In my weakest state, that is where the devil held my feet to the fire with my thoughts, my beliefs, and my faith….*"Do you really believe all that's true?"*

From within me, my spirit stood firm, dug in and it got very real. I prayed and asked for forgiveness for any sin and then for guidance out of the dark valley I was in. With a clear mind and conscience, I stood on my faith of the sacrifice that Christ made for all our sins and asked God to redeem me once again. I **"...Put [my] hope in the Lord, for with the Lord is unfailing love and with him is full redemption."**—Psalm 130:7

The devil surrounded me, unconvinced that my faith was strong enough. *"Do you really think He is coming?... if He even exists"*

My spirit bore down under the pressure. "He will send the help I need and rescue me from this disaster. I don't even know what help I need, but He does. I know He's coming because He said, **"Be strong and courageous. Do not be afraid or terrified because of them, for the Lord our God goes with you; he will Never leave you nor forsake you"** (Deuteronomy 31:6). I don't know when and I don't know how, but He will show up because **"God is not human, that he should lie, not a human being that he should change his mind"** (Numbers 23:19). If He doesn't come, then that scripture is a lie, and that means there is no real, living God. If there is no God, then there is no heaven or hell and we all just die."

As my spirit strengthened inside of me, I finished with "And if we all just die, you can kill me now. None of this pain or suffering is worth it if we just die. I don't even care about helping anyone else, because if they just turn into a pile of dust too when this is all over, what is the point? All this pain and suffering for nothing. Kill me now if God doesn't exist. No split second pleasure or joy in this blink of an eye life is worth the pain I have endured or watched others suffer!.......but if He does exist....

Now, it matters if I get up off this floor. Now, it matters if I try to purpose to do better. Now, there is meaning if I heal, if I can help others. It's a completely different story when I open my eyes and see the spiritual warfare all around us. I now become a warrior in a battle that matters for all of eternity. Now that is something I can stand on my faith and fight for."

Then my enemy came sharply into focus.

"For we do not wrestle against flesh and blood, but against principalities, against power, against the rulers of the darkness of this age, against spiritual hosts of wickedness in the heavenly places."
—(Ephesians 6:12)

I looked beyond my current situation. I let go of the need to find or place blame for what got me into my situation. I stopped looking for solutions in other people and temporary fixes for my pain. I focused my mind on the horizon, my destination that is eternity with Jesus, and my salvation that was given to me as a gift.

The divine energy that comes from knowing the truth of God began to flow over my spirit. I'm not quitting out of respect for God and everything He has done for me. Everything that I have in me goes on the line because it does matter what I choose to do now. The consequences of my choices are far-reaching.

My eyes fix their vision in the distance, and in my mind, any minute now...I expect to see or hear another rescue flight sent in by Jesus. He will get me out of this darkness. What shape or manner that comes in varies, but He will show up.

Sometimes it's a phone call from a friend, a kind word from a stranger, a random thought in my mind that distracts. Other times, I get just enough power back to alter my course. I stand back up, recalibrate my instruments, and my faith comes back on line enough to keep running my race.

* * *

If you should ever find yourself in spiritual darkness, know that there is always a way out with God. He will never leave you or forsake you (Hebrews 13:5). He has led me out of difficult situations many times. Even the ones that I have gotten myself into out of my own rebellion. He is a forgiving God. I urge you to keep trying to get better with the skills and resources He has given you and that await you at the next level of healing when you are ready.

Learning how to maintain your balance in life is a necessary skill we all need. By applying daily practice to master the use of scripture in your life, you can move forward in the plan that God has designed for you. Learning to hear his voice and course-correct is a Christian foundation that will bring you increased peace. Comprehending how to read the situations in your life and understand the people around you will bring you greater joy.

Realize that time keeps moving forward. You can opt out of training as long as you want, but you are missing out. A forgone opportunity means you are unprepared for the next journey God wants you to take. There could also be someone who is waiting on your help. We are all made to serve in some way.

No matter what your current circumstances are, you can begin to learn how to keep your peace, recover from hardship, and let God grow you into a deeper relationship of trust and understanding with Him.

You are practicing something every day. A decision to do nothing, is a decision. What are you getting better at doing? At least, be mindfully aware of the journey you are choosing to take and the skills you are mastering.

If you are suffering from inner turmoil, I hope the sharing of my experiences with God, gives Him glory as the caring redeemer He has always been for me and that it gives you inspiration that you too can get back up and flying again with His help.

Whatever your race may be, I hope this book serves as a witness and testimony of His enduring love, grace and power. May you hear His voice guiding you through each day.

May you have peace knowing that God is always with us and for us.

May that knowledge give you strength, hope and encouragement as you:

"...Run with endurance the race that is set before us"
—Hebrews 12:1

Conclusion
Vitality Tactics L.L.C.

As a life coach and a personal trainer, I want to you to know that I understand it is difficult to purpose to do better and stick with it. Maintaining your peace and keeping on target to your goals as you run your race in this life is not a simple undertaking. I have always felt my job as a trainer is to set others up for their next level of success by discovering and building more strength in themselves.

My natural inclination is to see a person's potential. I work with what I see they can be in the future, today. I set my expectations above what they are currently doing and encourage them to rise to the level they are capable of...and when they do, I am able to see their next frontier open up.

For me, the journey is never-ending and always changing. I have experienced that we have an endless stream of strength, energy and healing available to us through Jesus Christ. The ability to tap into that and explore what He has made us and called us to do is a vital tactic to living an abundant life.

A life with Christ opens up a world of adventure and joy. Learning how to recognize His presence and feel his guidance is an endless blessing. I hope this book helps you discover how to experience more of that each day.

You Are Going Somewhere, Get There with a Purpose

My question to you as you read this book, is where do you go from here? This book was written as a level one resource for Christians who are struggling to get out of darkness and find peace. However, the techniques and procedures discussed can help anyone move forward in the life they were meant to live. The use of scripture in your life offers a massive amount of power available to strengthen yourself and those around you.

Who is it you were created to be in this life? No matter where you are now, stop and take a minute to assess what is going to happen in 10, 20, or 30 years if you keep your current course. Are you in that place where you show up to heaven and hear:

"...Well done, good and faithful servant; you were faithful over a few things, I will make you ruler over many things. Enter into the joy of your lord."
—Matt 25:21

What will your relationships with God, your family and your friends look like ten years from now? Are you being the person you were designed to be and doing the work you were called to do?

What do you want to know you did when your time is up? I am not talking about a bucket list, but the relationship story you are writing about you and God for your time on this earth. Is it an adventure together? Or an estranged love story? You are the writer. You get to pick.

Through reading this book, I hope you find something that helps you learn how to make things better on your journey. I do not have a problem free life, I make mistakes, and still need flights out of the darkness sometimes. But they are needed less frequent, as time goes on. I recover more quickly, get stronger and wiser spiritually as time progresses. Make sure the techniques and tactics you are using are doing the same for you. I pray what I shared can help you refine your own strategies and #RunYourRace even better!

GodSpeed, Coach Onnie

Afterword

The following entries capture email conversations that took place during the editing phase:

--Your writing...has a factual presentation to it. You are putting pain on paper, that is apparent. The art of first person is fraught with exposure. This is a defense mechanism; emotional and psychological nudity is much more difficult than physical kind. The writing has a dispassionate quality and reasonably so. I am sure it is the only way to convey without emotion taking over.

I wanted to establish credibility about the subject by describing my times in deep depression without getting into the specifics of how I got there because I wanted to focus on the journey out. At this time, I did not find it necessary to speak about the specifics of the abuse that broke me into a destructive living pattern. Also, I am somewhat dissociated from what happened so it does come across as dis-

passionate. That is a residual behavior from narcisstic abuse. I was not allowed to be sad or depressed on the outside. Any accidental show of a negative emotion was met with ridicule or punishment. My pain was never valid. I was sometimes told I was making it up. I began to only recount events as factual in nature even when they hurt me deeply. I tried to rectify "why am I'm hurting if they did nothing wrong?" Then, I would turn it into a logic puzzle to take the pain away and focus on finding a solution.

--Are you mentally and spiritually prepared for public consumption and reaction?

Is anyone ever really?

--Is your family prepared for the same?

I have taken precautions to separate out certain things and create barriers for them.

--You need a backstory, does not need to reveal specifics on events:

I hesitate to give abuse details, because it distracts from my purpose of sharing how I got out. I do not feel the need to qualify my pain nor do I find it helpful to talk about it. I am a coach, we move things forward. That is my nature. Not saying I wouldn't reveal more later in a different story if it was needed or would be helpful to someone, but at this point I only want to focus on things that helped me get out of the trauma and destructive behaviors and choices. I want to help those still hurting. If anything in here can help at least one person find their way out, then it is worth it. It also gives my pain significance. Besides, my abusers are still alive and well. Some of them who label themselves "good people" who felt they have done no wrong. I have absorbed enough blame, guilt, and shame to justify their behavior. I do not wish to deal with them. I forgave them all to set myself free.

--Tell us about Onnie before event with worldview-optimistic, youthful, naive etc?

There is no prior time before traumatic events. I was born into destruction. Then raised in a sequence of abusive situations. I breathed fear in every day as a child. I dreamed, planned and worked hard on my escape out. There was no safety from what no one could see from the outside. No one tried to help me out because I was taught to hide my pain. I was told it didn't exist. I either kept fighting to stay out of the destruction that surrounded me and infiltrated my core, or I surrendered to the enemy in one of his forms: addiction, poverty, depression, etc. Those were my two choices.

--What about Onnie after these events with altered worldview. Did you feel betrayed, shattered, depressed, guarded etc?

The problem with answering this question is there is no one event. I have endured decades of betrayal from the very people who were supposed to love me or claimed they did. I just always had this feeling that...this can't be how this is supposed to be. Moments of feeling joy or peace before being pulled back into darkness, those captivated my mind. Never underestimate any act of kindness you do. In my life, any kind act or word shown to me has lifted my spirit and for a moment transported me to a place of hope. I have treasured every one of them as they restored my spirit so I could keep going.

--Therapy if any and effects, did you see light at the end, perseverance etc?

Cognitive therapy did give me small pieces of the puzzle. An outside perspective can help. One or two therapists helped me figure out a better technique to rewire my mind. However, finding a good therapist is like finding a needle in a haystack. For me, it wasn't worth the work to find a good one and then once I did, I quickly outgrew what they could provide in help. Although I am grateful for those aha! moments, they are often not life altering. They give you an adjustment to get closer to center. You must keep doing the work.

--Onnie on how to take on the future—don't let the bastards get you down?

Well, if I'm not going to end my journey of my own accord...I might as well figure out how to make this ride awesome. Depression can be very boring when it's not causing you immense pain.

--What are additional events that exacerbate the original wound and the compounding effects?

The list is long. Over the course of my life I have endured physical, emotional, sexual abuse and when the abusers were no longer present, I took over by treating myself terribly. I was what they call a type A addict. Nothing illegal or to the point it ever threatened my job or relationships. I used it to soothe pain and avoid the actual problems...because

I had no idea how to handle them... I find the recounting of that boring as well. I would rather tell the why and how of stopping and dealing with what caused me to misuse things and how to turn to God to heal.

--When did you hit bottom?

I was born there. I never remember not being afraid until I left home. It is more accurate to say that I have been on an upward trend for years. There are peaks and valleys, but overall, it keeps getting better.

--When was your Spiritual awakening?

I always knew there was a God. But one day I woke up and desperately needed Him to be a living, present God in my life. The inner turmoil in me was overwhelming at that point in my late 20's. It was a Joyce Meyers sermon that first revealed to me a present Jesus who was there to help me in my pain. She painted this picture of a God that could help me now, not only when I died and went to heaven. I have had my moments of doubt, but I chased those down. God designed us as intelligent, curious beings. It is not sinful to question his existence in a respectful manner. But I did the work of finding the information I needed to make a final decision. I found you need more faith to believe in science than God. After that decision, other ones become much easier.

*The most important question you answer for yourself in this life: Is Jesus Christ the son of God who came and died on the cross for your sins so you can have right standing with God and spend eternity in heaven?

*The most important decision you ever make in this life: Do you accept Him as your personal savior?

The answers to those questions decide your eternity...that is why they are the most important decisions you will ever make. One day I decided that I shouldn't take that lightly and I set out on my quest to be either all in, or out. I ended up going all in.

"A man with an experience of God is never at the mercy of a man with an argument"
—L. Ravenhill

Acknowledgements

To my first editor and dear friend Erykka, your contribution of time and emotional support far exceeded what should be asked of any person. You delivered in abundance. Your organization abilities of my thoughts were amazing and a blessing to have. I am struck with the idea that your skilled vision of the development of this book was in part due to our long-standing friendship and how well you know me. All possible because of a chance meeting in Jack's Valley over 20 years ago. "How curious"

To Colonel Heather, you are the best! Thank you for taking time out of your busy schedule to hack through my grammar, punctuation and provide feedback. I admire the light and spunk in your heart that time has never dulled. Your limitless energy to work for a greater cause than yourself, serve and lead those around you is inspirational.

To Chef, thanks for the insight. Still waiting to hear about the dream that sparked the email

To Angela, thank you for the encouragement I received when it passed your high standards of spiritual and intellectual quality. You will have to wait for level two for me to get into more specifics. I'm just not there yet. It will come.

To Mr. John: Sir, you have no idea how terrified I was to let you read this. The opinion of a well-respected, hard-working, mature Christian and great American, was much needed in giving me the confidence to go forward in publishing. Thank you so much for taking the time to read it and provide feedback.

To anyone who has encouraged me along the way, Thank You. Every positive word has given me another invaluable measure of hope.

And so it is done. The formation of this book started out as a vague desire planted in my heart and was pulled forth to the surface through fire. I was made to survive incredible amounts of emotional pain, learn from it, and teach others how to heal. It was not an easy path by any means and several times I almost chose not to keep going. I have my free-will and could have walked away like anyone else can from their purpose. But every time I started to, I looked over my shoulder and saw another person I could help. My disdain for attention, my inability to fight for only myself, and the fear of being attacked, those were all excuses. But there is no excuse for not helping others when you can. There is only the pain of living with your own chosen weakness. Looking back, it has been a gift to be made with ability to forge through the flames. The fortitude and grit that it has developed in me has taken me to amazing places and opportunities I would not have had otherwise. Healing both myself and others along the way. I never saw that part coming.

About the Author

Originally trained as a military pilot, Onnie Resky has enjoyed traveling around the world while serving in the Air Force and competing in Martial Arts and Ironman competitions. Initially labeled with depression while attending the U.S. Air Force Academy, Onnie pushed through the demanding academic and military requirements to graduate with the class of 1999. Through building athletic experience, expertise, and training others, Onnie began to notice and study the strong connections that our body, mind and spirit have and how they affect each other.

"As I would train the physical body of my clients or students, I would often find myself unexpectedly presented with the issues in their heart and mind. The physical stress would somehow cause their spirit or mind to speak out. After repeatedly finding myself in these moments, I felt I needed a tool to be able to handle these situations better. They needed more than just physical training. It alone was not enough to keep them moving towards and maintaining their goals even if the goal was only a physical one. I had to learn how to train all aspects of a person. Rewire their mind, strengthen the body and help them spiritually."

This led to seeking the training to become a certified Christian life coach. Then, by combining life coaching, athletic training and adding lessons learned fighting depression, Onnie developed training techniques to better incorporate our relationship with Christ to help fight one of the biggest epidemics of depression our society has ever experienced.

Ironman Finishes: Klagenfurt (Austria), Busselton (Western Australia), Zurich (Switzerland), Hokkaido (Japan), Vichy (France), Whistler (Canada), Panama City (U.S), Cozumel (Mexico), Florianopolis (Brazil) and Cambridge (U.S.)

Ironman 70.3 Finishes: Aarhus (Denmark), Zell Am See (Austria), Barcelona (Spain), Raleigh (U.S.), Haines City (U.S.)

3x Ironman All World Athlete: 2015-2017

3 x Continuous Sparring Champion World Organization of Martial Arts Athletes (W.O.M.A.A.): 2012-2013, 2015

SELF-PUBLISHING
SCHOOL

NOW IT'S YOUR TURN

Discover the EXACT 3-step blueprint you need to become a bestselling author in 3 months.

Self-Publishing School helped me, and now I want them to help you with this FREE WEBINAR!

Even if you're busy, bad at writing, or don't know where to start, you CAN write a bestseller and build your best life.

With tools and experience across a variety niches and professions, Self-Publishing School is the <u>only</u> resource you need to take your book to the finish line!

DON'T WAIT

Watch this FREE WEBINAR now, and Say "YES" to becoming a bestseller:

https://xe172.isrefer.com/go/affegwebinar/ bookbrosinc6938/

Made in the USA
Columbia, SC
30 September 2019